WHEREVER
YOU GO,
THERE
YOU ARE

Also by Jon Kabat-Zinn:

*Mindfulness Meditation for Pain Relief: Practices to
Reclaim Your Body and Your Life*

Mindfulness for All: The Wisdom to Transform the World

The Healing Power of Mindfulness: A New Way of Being

Falling Awake: How to Practice Mindfulness in Everyday Life

*Meditation Is Not What You Think: Mindfulness and
Why It Is So Important*

*Mindfulness: Diverse Perspectives on Its Meaning,
Origins, and Applications*
(editor, with J. Mark G. Williams)

*Mindfulness for Beginners: Reclaiming the Present
Moment—and Your Life*

*The Mind's Own Physician: A Scientific Dialogue with the Dalai Lama
on the Healing Power of Meditation* (editor, with Richard J. Davidson)

Letting Everything Become Your Teacher: 100 Lessons in Mindfulness

Arriving at Your Own Door: 108 Lessons in Mindfulness

*The Mindful Way Through Depression: Freeing Yourself
from Chronic Unhappiness*
(with Mark Williams, John Teasdale, and Zindel Segal)

*Coming to Our Senses: Healing Ourselves and the
World Through Mindfulness*

Everyday Blessings: The Inner Work of Mindful Parenting
(with Myla Kabat-Zinn)

*Full Catastrophe Living: Using the Wisdom of Your Body and
Mind to Face Stress, Pain, and Illness*

30TH ANNIVERSARY EDITION

WHEREVER YOU GO, THERE YOU ARE

Mindfulness Meditation in Everyday Life

A Guide to Your Place in the Universe and an Inquiry into Who and What You Are

Jon Kabat-Zinn

hachette
BOOKS

New York

Copyright © 1994, 2005, 2023 by Jon Kabat-Zinn
Cover design and illustration by Holly Ovenden
Cover copyright © 2023 by Hachette Book Group, Inc.

Hachette Go, an imprint of Hachette Books
Hachette Book Group
1290 Avenue of the Americas
New York, NY 10104
HachetteGo.com
Facebook.com/HachetteGo
Instagram.com/HachetteGo

Revised Edition: December 2023

Originally published in hardcover by Hyperion.

Published by Hachette Go, an imprint of Hachette Book Group, Inc. The Hachette Go name and logo is a trademark of the Hachette Book Group.

The Hachette Speakers Bureau provides a wide range of authors for speaking events. To find out more, go to hachettespeakersbureau.com or email HachetteSpeakers@hbgusa.com.

Hachette Go books may be purchased in bulk for business, educational, or promotional use. For information, please contact your local bookseller or Hachette Book Group Special Markets Department at: special.markets@hbgusa.com.

The publisher is not responsible for websites (or their content) that are not owned by the publisher.

Library of Congress Cataloging-in-Publication Data

Names: Kabat-Zinn, Jon, author.
Title: Wherever you go, there you are: mindfulness meditation in everyday life /
    Jon Kabat-Zinn.
Description: 30th anniversary edition. | New York, NY : Hachette Go, 2023. |
    Originally published in hardcover by Hyperion.
Identifiers: LCCN 2023030644 | ISBN 9780306832017 (paperback) | ISBN 9780306832024 (ebook)
Subjects: LCSH: Meditation. | Attention.
Classification: LCC BF637.M4 K23 2023 | DDC 158.1/2—dc23/eng/20230717
LC record available at https://lccn.loc.gov/2023030644

ISBNs: 978-0-306-83201-7 (paperback), 978-0-306-83202-4 (ebook)

Printed in the United States of America

LSC-C

Printing 2, 2024

For Myla—love beyond words

For Will, Naushon, Serena, Toby, Asa, Stella,
and Joaquim, wherever you go

In memory of Aunt M, a.k.a. Maureen Stafford, physician,
bodhisattva, mother, grandmother, children's book incessant
gifter and inscriber, mindfulness teacher, blessing to the world

and

With a deep Dharma bow to dedicated mindfulness teachers
and practitioners everywhere

Contents

PART THREE: In the Spirit of Mindfulness

Introduction to the 30th Anniversary Edition

Although this book is not even remotely about the science of mindfulness or its clinical applications, I have noticed over the decades that it continues to be widely cited in the scientific and medical literature, and always and only for one particular detail: the working definition I offered in the original 1994 edition to explain what mindfulness actually is in operational terms to those who had no firsthand familiarity with it through formal meditative cultivation—which in those days was almost everybody. I described it as *the awareness that arises from paying attention on purpose, in the present moment, and nonjudgmentally.* And if there was a need to explain *why* one might be drawn to cultivate greater mindfulness, the following phrase could be added (as I did in the introduction to *Meditation Is Not What You Think* in 2018): *". . . in the service of wisdom, self-understanding, and recognizing our intrinsic interconnectedness with others and with the world, and thus, also in the service of kindness and compassion."* Taking a cue from the poignant genius of Greta Thunberg, I feel it is totally appropriate to recognize human awareness as a superpower, one we all already possess by virtue of being human. But for the most part, this superpower remains unrecognized and untapped by humanity—we get virtually no instruction in mainstream culture for how it might be accessed, inhabited, and put to use. That now has to change on a global level, and relatively quickly, if we are to realize our full potential as a species and live up to the name we have accorded ourselves: *Homo sapiens sapiens*—the species that is aware, and is aware that it is aware—or more in line with modern psychological terminology, awareness and meta-awareness. Time to wake up, maybe long past time. And there is only one time that it can ever happen. Can you guess when that might be? This is an "all-hands-on-deck-on-Spaceship-Earth" moment, to hark back to Buckminster Fuller's more-timely-than-ever phrase from circa 1969. The Dharma, in all its simplicity and complexity and universality, has never been more necessary for human and planetary flourishing.

On September 11, 2001, the Japanese Zen master Harada Roshi was teaching at his American center on Whidbey Island in Puget Sound. Myla and I happened to be on the island leading a workshop on mindful parenting the night before. Everything in the entire country came to a stop the next morning as we learned about the attacks of that day. Gray warships emerged out of the fog patrolling the straights. Harada extended an invitation to a number of people in the community to visit with him that day—a welcome respite from watching the Twin Towers fall over and over again on the news. When we were leaving, he gave each of us present a poster, an *enso*—a calligraphic one-brushstroke Zen circle—underneath which it said, in English: *Never forget the one-thousand-year view.* Unwritten but not unrecognized was the poignant probability that we may not have one thousand years. The need for us to wake up to our true nature and potential as human beings has never been greater, nor its likelihood more favorable, given the accelerated spread of an ever-more-diverse and accessible universal Dharma wisdom around the world, now, increasingly accessible to all via the internet. In a very real way, the cultivation of mindfulness as both a liberative formal meditation practice and, not separately, as a Way of being—in which life itself and how we live it moment by moment by moment becomes the real meditation practice—takes on the characteristics of a selfless love affair and an expression of everything that is deepest and best in our nature as human beings.

In my vocabulary, "mindfulness" is synonymous with "awareness," pure and simple. But although it is our birthright, and right under our noses, so to speak, all puns intended, we have little access to this superpower in a reliable way. Mindfulness meditation is a way to cultivate that access, so that pure embodied awareness, or wakefulness, can become our default mode, the ground of our being, and a trustworthy guide to how we might carry ourselves through life to optimize well-being for ourselves, for each other, for all living creatures, and for our world, and to minimize delusion and suffering wherever possible.

Here is a little story at the very root of the Zen/Chan Buddhist meditation tradition that might give you a little taste of the wisdom of pure awareness from a non-dual perspective, essential for any deep and embodied understanding of what mindfulness is and isn't:

Hui-neng (638–713), an illiterate woodcutter, had a very strong inclination toward the Dharma of awakening. As a teenager, he overheard a monk reciting the Diamond Sutra, and one line immediately struck him to his core: "Develop a mind that clings to nothing." Sometimes it is translated as "Develop a mind that abides nowhere." On the spot, his mind opened. He left home and sought out the monastery of the fifth Chan patriarch, Hongren, working as a lowly rice pounder in the kitchen. After eight months, the master let it be known among the sangha of one thousand monks that he wished to pass on to a successor the robe and bowl emblematic of his authority and understanding. He invited anyone who cared to to post a statement of their understanding of the essence of Chan/Dharma on the monastery wall so that all could apprehend its wisdom. Shenxiu, the most learned of his disciples and widely considered by the monastics to be the only possible candidate to receive transmission from the master, posted the following:

> *This body is the Bodhi-tree,** *
> *The mind a mirror bright;*
> *Take heed to brush it always clean,*
> *And let no dust alight.*

Hearing these verses recited by a young acolyte passing by the threshing room window, the lowly rice pounder knew immediately that they were off the mark. Being illiterate, he asked the boy to take him to the wall in the front hall of the monastery and recite it for him again. Hui-neng then asked a passing temple administrator whether he, Hui-neng, could also offer a verse to be put on the wall. The astonished administrator agreed to write it for him. His offering went like this:

---

* *Bodhi* means "awakening" or "enlightenment."

Basically, bodhi has no tree,
Nor is it a mirror bright,
Originally there is not one thing,
Where could dust alight?

Needless to say, his succinct encapsulation demonstrated the profundity of his understanding of non-duality and the empty nature of what we refer to as self, meaning that one cannot locate a fixed, separate, unchanging entity within the domain of name and form, or beyond the domain of name and form, for that matter. So, of course, the lowly rice pounder received the robe and the bowl, symbolic of that direct transmission from one awakened mind/ heart to another, and thus became the sixth, and last, Chan patriarch. But the ceremony had to take place in secret, with no witnesses, because the retiring Hongren knew that the jealous monks, in spite of all their practice of compassion, might wish the young man harm. Hui-neng left in the night, carrying with him not only the robe and begging bowl emblematic of the transmission but the embodied realization of the non-self-centered nature of pure awareness, or put differently, of wakefulness, at the heart of the meditation practice—a nature that transcends both the necessarily *instrumental* time-bound aspect of meditation practice on a relative, conventional level—where the more you practice, the more "progress" you make toward some desirable goal—and the more essential, non-instrumental dimension of meditation practice where embodied wakefulness is already here and constitutes the true nature of human awareness. It is both boundless and timeless, and it is already yours, in the sense of being a core signature of being human.* This remarkable meditative wisdom lineage continued unbroken for several centuries in China, giving rise to a flowering of Dharma in the Tang and Song dynasties and to expressions of cultural, artistic, and philosophical wisdom second to none on the planet. And that Chan energy is very much alive to this day and resurgent around the world as part of an explosion of interest in mindfulness, including in present-day China.

The Buddha originally described mindfulness as "the direct path to realization," to liberation from greed, hatred, and delusion, and the selfing and suffering that follow in their wake. As you will see and hopefully *feel* as a transmission of sorts from these pages—from the words and the spaces between them, inside them, and underneath them, directly into your heart—mindfulness is both a formal meditation practice and a Way of being.

If what follows speaks to you, my hope is that the practice of mindfulness as described here will be wholeheartedly welcomed by you, entered into, and taken up for life, for your own sake, the sake of your loved ones, and for the sake of the world. May it enliven your moments as your unique and precious life, not to be missed or underestimated, continues to unfold.

---

* See J. Kabat-Zinn, "Two Ways to Think About Meditation—the Instrumental and the Non-Instrumental," in *Meditation Is Not What You Think*, Hachette, 2018, 49–53.

Introduction to the First Edition

Guess what? When it comes right down to it, wherever you go, there you are. Whatever you wind up doing, that's what you've wound up doing. Whatever you are thinking right now, *that's* what's on your mind. Whatever has happened to you, it has already happened. The important question is, how are you going to be in wise relationship to it? In other words, "Now what?"

Like it or not, this moment is all we really have to work with. Yet we all too easily conduct our lives as if forgetting momentarily that we are *here*, where we already are, and that we are *in* what we are already in. In every moment, we find ourselves at the crossroads of here and now. But when the cloud of forgetfulness over where we are now sets in, in that very moment we get lost. "Now what?" becomes a real problem.

By lost, I mean that we momentarily lose touch with ourselves and with the full extent of our possibilities. Instead, we fall into a robot-like way of seeing and thinking and doing. In those moments, we break contact with what is deepest in ourselves and that affords us perhaps our greatest opportunities for creativity and for ongoing learning, growing, and healing. If we are not careful, those clouded moments can stretch out and become most of our lives.

To allow ourselves to be truly in touch with where we already are, no matter where that is, we have got to pause in our experience long enough to let the present moment sink in—long enough to actually *feel* the present moment, to see it in its fullness, to inhabit it and hold it in awareness, and thereby come to know and understand it better, with greater intimacy and appreciation. Only then can we accept the truth of this moment of our life, learn from it, and move on. Instead, it often seems as if we are preoccupied with the past, with what has already happened, or with a future that hasn't arrived yet. We look for someplace else to stand, where we hope things will be better, happier, more the way we want them to be or the way they used to be. Most of the time we are only partially aware of this inner tension, if we are aware of it at all. What is more, we are also only partially aware at best of exactly what we are doing in and with our lives, and the effects our actions and, more subtly, our thoughts and emotions have on what we see and don't see, what we do and don't do.

For instance, we usually fall, quite unawares, into assuming that what we are thinking—the ideas and opinions that we harbor at any given time—is "the truth" about what is "out there" in the world and "in here" in our minds. Most of the time, it just isn't so.

We pay a high price for this mistaken and unexamined assumption, for our almost willful ignoring of the richness of our present moments. The fallout accumulates silently, coloring our lives without our knowing it or being able to do something about it. We may never quite be where we actually are, never quite touch the fullness of our possibilities. Instead, we lock ourselves into a personal fiction that we already know who we are, that we know where we are and where we are going, that we know what is happening—all the while remaining enshrouded in thoughts, fantasies, and impulses, mostly about the past and about the future, about what we want and like, and what we fear and don't like, which spin out continuously, veiling our direction and the very ground we are standing on.

The book you have in your hands is about waking up from such dreams and from the nightmares they often turn into. Not knowing that you are even in such a dream is what the Buddhist tradition refers to as "ignorance," or mindlessness. Being in touch with this not-knowing is called "mindfulness." The work of waking up from these dreams is the work of meditation, the systematic cultivation of wakefulness, of present-moment awareness. This waking up goes hand in hand with what we might call "wisdom," seeing more deeply into cause and effect and the interconnectedness of things, so that we are no longer caught in a dream-dictated reality of our own creation. To find our way, we will need to pay more attention to this moment. It is the only time that we have in which to live, grow, feel, and change. We will need to become more aware of and take precautions against the incredible pull of the Scylla and Charybdis of past and future, and the dreamworlds they offer us in place of our lives.

When we speak of meditation, it is important for you to know that this is not some weird cryptic activity, as some currents in our popular culture might have it. It does not involve becoming some kind of zombie, self-absorbed narcissist, navel gazer, cultist, devotee, mystic, or Eastern philosopher. Meditation is simply about being yourself and knowing something about who that is. It is about coming to realize that you are on a path whether you like it or not; namely, the path that is your life. Meditation may help us see that this path we call our life has direction; that it is always unfolding, moment by moment; and that what happens now, in this moment, influences what happens next.

If what happens now does influence what happens next, then doesn't it make sense to look around a bit from time to time so that you are more in touch with what is happening now, so that you can take your inner and outer bearings and perceive with clarity the path that you are actually on and the direction in which you are going? If you do so, maybe you will be in a better position to chart a course for yourself that is truer to and more in alignment with your inner being—a path with heart, *your* Path with a capital *P*. If not, the sheer momentum of your unconsciousness in this moment just colors the next moment. The days, months, and years quickly go by unnoticed, unused, unappreciated.

It is all too easy to remain on something of a fog-enshrouded, slippery slope right into our graves—or, in the fog-dispelling clarity that on occasion precedes the moment of death, to wake up and realize that what we had thought all those years about how life was to be lived and what was important were at best unexamined half-truths based on fear or ignorance, only our own life-limiting ideas, and not the truth or the way our life had to be at all.

No one else can do this job of waking up for us, although our family and friends do sometimes try desperately to get through to us, to help us see more clearly or break out of our own opaque rigidity and blindnesses. But waking up is ultimately something that each one of us can only do for ourselves. When it comes down to it, wherever *you* go, there *you* are. It's your life that is unfolding.

At the end of a long life dedicated to teaching mindfulness, the Buddha, who probably had his share of followers who were hoping he might make it easier for them to find their own paths, summed it up for his disciples this way: "Be a light unto yourself."

Of course, the universe is always available to collaborate in illuminating the actuality of things. You need to be a light unto yourself. But you are also not alone, even if you sometimes feel that way. Like all life, you are an intimate part of larger and larger circles of belonging.

In my first book, *Full Catastrophe Living*, I tried to make the path of mindfulness accessible to mainstream Americans so that it would not feel Buddhist or mystical so much as commonsensical. Mindfulness has to do above all with attention and awareness, which are universal human qualities. But in our society, we tend to take these capacities for granted and don't think to develop them systematically in the service of self-understanding and wisdom. Meditation is the process by which we go about refining our attention and familiarizing ourselves with awareness by learning how to inhabit it, thus putting both attention and awareness to much greater practical and potentially healing and transformative use in our lives and in our relationships with the world.

Full Catastrophe Living can be thought of as a navigational chart of sorts, the curriculum of mindfulness-based stress reduction (MBSR), intended for people facing physical or emotional pain and illness or reeling from the effects of too much stress. The aim was to challenge the reader to realize, through their direct experience of paying attention to things we all so often ignore, that there might be very real and beneficial reasons, including optimizing one's physical, mental, and social health, for integrating mindfulness as a formal meditation practice and as a Way of being into the fabric of one's life. Thinking back to conditions in the United States and the rest of the world in 1979, when MBSR began at the University of Massachusetts Medical Center in Worcester, Massachusetts, the idea that Americans would take up and adhere to authentic and life-long meditation practice at a population level was akin to insane. Yet it has come about, and MBSR programs are now available in person, as well as online, throughout much of the world. From the beginning, the aim was to, over time, help move the bell curve of society as a whole toward greater levels of wellbeing, embod-ied wakefulness, and flourishing, not as a form of therapy, but as a public health intervention on a national and potentially even global scale. At the time, it was seen by some in medicine as madness—the Visigoths were at the gates of the citadel of Western civilization and scientific medicine, about to destroy it with meditative, mystical nonsense—yet it is increasingly coming about as part of an ever-expanding view and understanding of what it means to be human, and none too soon, in my view.

Not that I was suggesting that mindfulness is some kind of a cure-all or dime-store solution to life's problems. Far from it. I don't know of any magical solutions, and, frankly, I am not looking for one. A full life is painted with broad brush strokes. Many paths can lead to understanding, to a life of greater wisdom and compassion. Each of us has different needs to address and things worth pursuing over the course of a lifetime. Each of us has to chart our own course, and it has to fit what we are ready for and what we aspire to.

You certainly have to be ready for formal meditation practice. It takes time to implement. It takes resolve to practice every day. It takes a significant degree of discipline. You have to come to it at the right time in your life, at a point where you are ready to listen carefully to your own voice, to your own heart, to your own breathing—to just be present for them and with them, without having to go anywhere or make anything better or different. This is hard work.

I was moved to write *Full Catastrophe Living* after years of witnessing the sometimes remarkable transformations in mind and body that many people reported as they put aside trying to change the severe problems that brought them to the Stress Reduction Clinic and, instead, engaged together over those eight weeks in the intensive discipline of opening and listening that characterizes the practice of mindfulness—of actually putting out the welcome mat, you might say, for things as they are, however they are.

As a navigational chart, *Full Catastrophe Living* had to supply enough detail so that someone in significant need could plot their own course with care. It had to speak to the pressing needs of people with serious medical conditions and chronic pain, as well as to those suffering the health effects, mental and physical and social, from different kinds of stressful life situations. For these reasons, that book had to include a good deal of information on stress and illness, health and healing, the science of mindfulness, as well as extensive instructions on how to meditate and implement a disciplined formal meditation practice.

This book is different. It aims to provide brief and easy access to the essence of mindfulness meditation and its applications for people whose lives may or may not be dominated by immediate problems of stress, pain, and illness, although in the end, we all are to one degree or another. This book is offered particularly for those who resist structured programs and for people who don't like to be told what to do but are curious enough about mindfulness and its relevance to try to piece things together for themselves with a few hints and suggestions here and there.

At the same time, this book is also offered to those who are already practicing meditators and wish to expand, deepen, and reinforce their commitment to a life of greater awareness and insight. Here, in brief chapters, the focus is on the spirit of mindfulness, both in our formal attempts to practice and in our efforts to bring it into all aspects of our everyday lives. Each chapter is an offering, a glimpse through one face of the multifaceted diamond of mindfulness. The chapters are related to each other by tiny rotations of the crystal. Some may sound similar to others, but each facet is also different, unique.

This exploration of the diamond of mindfulness is offered for all those who would chart a course toward greater sanity and wisdom in their lives and, by extension, for all those who also wish to be of benefit to the wider world. What is required is a willingness to look deeply at one's present moments, no matter what they hold, in a spirit of generosity and kindness toward oneself, and openness toward what might be possible.

Part One explores the rationale and background for taking on or deepening a personal practice of mindfulness. It challenges you to experiment with introducing mindfulness into your life in a number of different ways. Part Two explores some basic aspects of formal meditation practice. Formal practice refers to specific periods of time in which we purposefully stop other activity and engage in particular meditative practices for cultivating mindfulness and inhabiting the "space" of awareness in relatively stable and embodied ways—making room for increasing degrees of clarity and equanimity to arise. It emphasizes that "taking one's seat," both literally and metaphorically in sitting meditation, as well as in other postures, is taking a stand in one's life, and is ultimately a radical act of sanity and love. Part Three explores a range of applications and perspectives on mindfulness and, most importantly, emphasizes that life itself is the real meditation practice. Certain chapters in all three parts end with explicit suggestions for incorporating aspects of both formal and informal mindfulness practice into one's life. They are found under the heading "TRY." You are encouraged to explore these offerings seriously, and also playfully.

This volume contains sufficient instructions to engage in meditation practice on one's own, without the use of other materials or supports. However, many people find it helpful to make use of guidance through various audio devices, especially at the beginning, to support the daily discipline of a formal meditation practice and guide them in the instructions until they get the hang of it and wish to practice more on their own. Others find that even after years of meditation practice, it is helpful on occasion to make use of guided meditations. Originally, a series of guided meditations (Series 2) was specifically developed to be used in conjunction with this book. These practices range in length from ten minutes to half an hour; they give the reader who is new to formal mindfulness meditation practice a range of approaches to experiment with, as well as room to decide what length of formal practice is appropriate for a given time and place. These guided meditations are accessible in a range of ways, including in the JKZ Meditations app, where they are called *Everyday Life Meditations*, or as downloads. Links to these resources can be found at the back of the book.

PART ONE

The Bloom of the Present Moment

Only that day dawns to which we are awake.

HENRY DAVID THOREAU, *Walden*

What Is Mindfulness?

Mindfulness is an ancient Buddhist practice that has compelling relevance for our present-day lives. This relevance has nothing to do with Buddhism per se or with becoming a Buddhist, but it has everything to do with waking up and finding authentic ways to live in dynamic and creative harmony with oneself and with the world. It has to do with examining who we are, with questioning our view of the world and our place in it, and with cultivating some appreciation for the fullness of each precious moment in which we are alive. Most of all, it has to do with being present, with recognizing and being more in touch with the depths of your original mind and heart, and with being a locus of sanity and kindness in a sometimes very crazy and painful world.

From the Buddhist perspective, our ordinary waking consciousness is seen as severely suboptimal, both limited and limiting, resembling in many respects an extended dream rather than wakefulness. Meditation helps us wake up from this sleep of automaticity and unconsciousness, thereby making it possible for us to live our lives with access to the full spectrum of our conscious and unconscious possibilities. Monastics, sages, yogis, and Zen masters, women and men, have been exploring this territory systematically for thousands of years; in the process they have learned something that may now be profoundly beneficial for humanity to adopt on a global scale to counterbalance the prevailing orientation toward controlling and subduing nature rather than honoring that we are an intimate part of it. Their collective experience over the centuries suggests that by investigating inwardly and befriending our own truest, most authentic nature as human beings and—to be more specific—the nature of our own minds and hearts through careful and systematic attending, we may be able to live lives of greater satisfaction, harmony, and wisdom, and be of significant benefit to others and, at this critical moment in time, to the larger world and planet Earth itself. It also proffers a view of the world that is complementary to the predominantly reductionist and material-istic one currently dominating Western thought and institutions. This view is neither particularly "Eastern" nor mystical. Tho-reau saw the same problem with our ordinary mind state in New England in 1846 and wrote with great passion about its unfortunate consequences.

Mindfulness has been called the heart of Buddhist meditation. Its power lies in its practice and its applications. In my vocabulary, "mindfulness" is synonymous with pure awareness. It is a profound inborn human capacity. You already have it. We all do. Or perhaps it would be more accurate to say we *are* it, as it is such a fundamen-tal element of our nature as human beings. So there is nothing to get here, except perhaps out of our own way, so that easy access to the spaciousness of awareness emerges on its own.

We can access awareness (I won't say "our" awareness, because it is neither accurate nor appropriate to be possessive about it), as noted earlier, by paying attention in a particular way: on purpose, in the present moment, and non-judgmentally. Paying attention in this way gives us immediate access to awareness itself. And learning to "inhabit" or "take up residency in" awareness naturally invites greater wellbeing, clarity, compassion, insight, meaning, and a palpable sense of interconnectedness into present-moment experience, what we sometimes refer to as "reality."

The systematic cultivation of mindfulness through formal meditation practices wakes us up to the fact that our lives unfold only in moments. If we are not fully present for many of those moments, we may not only miss what is most valuable in our lives but also fail to realize the richness and the depth of our possibilities for growth and transformation—often in the very next moment—along with a profound coming to terms with things as they are, which is my working definition of healing, and as you will see, has nothing to do with passive resignation.

A diminished awareness of the present moment inevitably creates other problems for us as well, through our unconscious and automatic actions and behaviors, often driven by deep-seated fears and insecurities. These tend to grow bigger and more problematic if they are not welcomed in and attended to, eventually leaving us feeling stuck and out of touch. Over time, we may lose confidence in our ability to redirect our energies in ways that would lead to greater personal satisfaction and happiness, and perhaps even to greater health, and to a deeper sense of meaning and connection and agency in regard to the larger world.

Mindfulness as both a formal meditation practice and as a way of being in the world provides a simple but powerful route for getting ourselves unstuck, back in touch with our own intrinsic wisdom and vitality. It is a way to take charge of the direction and quality of our own lives, including our relationships within the family, our relationship to work and to the larger world and planet, and most fundamentally, our relationship, each one of us, with ourself as a person.

The key to this path, which lies at the root of Buddhism, Taoism, and yoga, and which we also find in the works of people like Emerson, Thoreau, and Whitman, and in Native American and other Indigenous wisdom traditions worldwide, is an appreciation for the present moment and the cultivation of an intimate relationship with it through a continual attending to it with care and discernment. It is the direct opposite of taking life for granted.

The habit of ignoring our present moments in favor of others yet to come leads directly to a pervasive lack of awareness of the web of life in which we are embedded. This includes a lack of awareness and understanding of our own mind and how it influences our perceptions and our actions. It severely limits our perspective on what it means to be a person and how we are connected to each other and to the world around us. Religion has traditionally been the domain of such fundamental inquiries within a spiritual framework, but mindfulness has little to do with religion, except in the most fundamental meaning of the word, as an attempt to appreciate the deep mystery of being alive and to acknowledge being vitally and intimately connected to all that exists.

When we commit ourselves to paying attention in an open way—and thus perhaps to being a bit more aware of the tendency to fall prey to our own likes and dislikes, opinions and prejudices, projections and expectations—new possibilities open up, and we have a chance to free ourselves from the straitjacket of endemic unconsciousness.

You might think of mindfulness simply as the art of conscious living. You don't have to be a Buddhist or a yogi to practice it. In fact, if you know anything about Buddhism, you will know that the most important point is to be yourself and not try to become anything that you are not already. Buddhism is fundamentally about being in touch with your own deepest nature and letting it flow out of you unimpeded. It has to do with waking up and seeing things as they are. In fact, the word "Buddha" simply means one who is awake to the actuality of things, including to the beauty of one's own truest, deepest nature.

So, mindfulness will not conflict with any beliefs or traditions—religious or for that matter scientific—nor is it trying to sell you anything, especially not a new belief system or ideology. It is simply a practical way to be more in touch with the fullness of your being through a systematic process of observation, inquiry, and mindful action. There is nothing cold, analytical, or unfeeling about it. The overall tenor of mindfulness practice is gentle, appreciative, and nurturing. Another way to think of it would be "heartfulness."

*

A student once said: "When I was a Buddhist, it drove my parents and friends crazy, but when I am a buddha, nobody is upset at all."

Simple but Not Easy

Although it may be simple to practice mindfulness, it is not necessarily easy. Mindfulness requires effort and discipline for the simple reason that the forces that work against our being mindful—namely, our habitual unawareness and automaticity—are exceedingly tenacious. They are so strong and so much out of our consciousness that an inner commitment and a certain kind of work are necessary just to keep up our attempts to capture our moments in awareness and sustain some degree of mindfulness over time. But it is an intrinsically satisfying work because it puts us in touch with many aspects of our lives that are habitually overlooked and lost to us.

It is also enlightening and liberating work. It is enlightening in that it literally allows us to see more clearly, and therefore come to understand more deeply, areas in our lives that we were out of touch with or unwilling to look at. This may include encountering deep emotions—such as grief, loneliness, sadness, woundedness, anger, and fear—that we might not ordinarily allow ourselves to intentionally hold in awareness or express consciously, and ultimately, to befriend and learn how to metabolize so they don't erode our wellbeing. Mindfulness can also help us to recognize and appreciate feelings such as joy, wellbeing, awe and wonder, peacefulness, and happiness that so often go by fleetingly and unacknowledged. It is liberating in that it leads to new ways of being in our own skin and in the world that can free us from the habit-dug ruts we so often fall into so unwittingly. It is also empowering, because paying attention in this way opens channels to deep reservoirs of creativity, intelligence, imagination, clarity, determination, agency, compassion, and wisdom within us.

One salient characteristic of our lives that we tend to be particularly unaware of is that we are thinking virtually all the time. The incessant stream of thoughts flowing through our minds leaves us very little respite for inner quiet. And we leave precious little room for ourselves anyway just to be, without having to run around doing things all the time. Our actions are all too frequently driven, rather than undertaken in awareness—driven by those perfectly ordinary thoughts and impulses that run through the mind like a coursing river, if not a waterfall. We get caught up in the torrent, and it winds up submerging our lives as it carries us to places we may not wish to go and may not even realize we are headed for.

Meditation means learning how to get out of this current, sit by its bank, and listen to it, learn from it, and then use its energies to guide us rather than to tyrannize and imprison us. This learning trajectory doesn't magically unfold all by itself. It takes energy. We call the effort to cultivate greater access to our ability to dwell in the present moment *practice* or, more formally, *meditation practice*. In the end, as you will see, the real meditation practice becomes coextensive with life itself—a love affair with what is most precious and most easily missed.

*

Question: How can I set right a tangle that is entirely below the level of my consciousness?

Nisargadatta: By being with yourself...by watching yourself in your daily life with alert interest, with the intention to understand rather than to judge, in full acceptance of whatever may emerge, because it is there, you encourage the deep to come to the surface and enrich your life and consciousness with its captive energies. This is the great work of awareness; it removes obstacles and releases energies by understanding the nature of life and mind. Intelligence is the door to freedom and alert attention is the mother of intelligence.

NISARGADATTA MAHARAJ, *I Am That*

Stopping

People think of meditation as some kind of special activity, but this is not exactly correct. Meditation is simplicity itself. As a joke, we sometimes say: "Don't just do something, sit there." But meditation is not just about sitting, either. It is about stopping and being present, that is all—not filling up our moments with anything. Mostly we run around doing. Are you able to come to a stop in your life, even for one moment? Could it be *this* moment? What would happen if you did?

A good way to free yourself, at least momentarily, from the incessant doing is to shift into "being mode" for a moment. You can play with it right now. Picture yourself as a boundless and timeless field of awareness, centered in the body, effortlessly apprehending this moment in its fullness, without trying to intercede or change anything at all. What is happening right here, right now? What do you feel? What do you see? What do you hear? How do you know any of this?

The funny thing about stopping is that as soon as you do it, here you are. Things get simpler. In some ways, it's as if you died and the world continued on. If you did die, all your responsibilities and obligations would immediately evaporate. Their residue would somehow get worked out without you. No one else can take over your unique agenda. It would die or peter out with you just as it has for everyone else who has ever died. So you don't need to worry about it in any absolute way.

If this is true, maybe right in this moment you don't need to check your phone or some other device, or distract yourself in any other way, even if you think you do. Maybe you don't need to pick up something to read in this moment, or run one more errand, or send one more text or email. By taking a few moments to "die on purpose" to the rush of time while you are still living, you free yourself to have time for the present. By "dying" now to the past and the future in this way, you actually become more alive, realizing that this moment is the only moment available to you—or to any of us, ever. Why not inhabit it while you have the chance, and see what unfolds in the here and now?

This is what stopping can do. There is nothing passive about it. And when you decide to go, it's a different kind of going because you stopped. The stopping actually makes the going more vivid, richer, more textured. It helps keep all the things we worry about and feel inadequate about in perspective. It provides a reliable and trustworthy coordinate system. It gives us useful navigational guidance as life unfolds moment by moment by timeless moment.

TRY: Stopping, sitting down, and becoming aware of your breathing (that is, the sensations of breathing in the body, wherever they are most vivid for you) once in a while throughout the day. It can be for five minutes, or even five seconds. Let go into full acceptance of the present moment, including how you are feeling and what you perceive to be happening. For these moments, don't try to change anything at all, just breathe and let go. Breathe and let be. Die to having to have anything be different in this moment; in your mind and in your heart, give yourself permission to allow this moment to be exactly as it is, and allow yourself to be exactly as you are. Recognize that in a very real way, the body is doing the breathing, not you. It is more like you are being breathed than that it is you, whoever you think you are, who is doing the breathing. The brainstem, the phrenic nerve, and the diaphragm are collaborating in a continuous symphony to keep you alive 24/7, when you are asleep as well as when you are awake. So you can simply give yourself over to *experiencing* the actual sensations in the body of this breath coming in, this breath going out, all on their own, without any pushing or pulling of the breath.

Then, when you're ready, move in the direction your heart tells you to go, mindfully and with resolve, noticing perhaps from time to time that the breath moves with you.

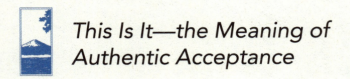

This Is It—the Meaning of Authentic Acceptance

New Yorker cartoon: Two Zen monks in robes and with shaved heads, one young, one old, sitting side by side cross-legged on the floor. The younger one is looking somewhat quizzically at the older one, who is turned toward him and saying, "Nothing happens next. This is it."

It's true. Ordinarily, when we undertake something, it is only natural to expect a desirable outcome for our efforts. We want to see results, even if it is only a pleasant feeling. The sole exception I can think of is meditation. Meditation is the only intentional, systematic human activity that at bottom is about *not* trying to improve yourself or get somewhere else but simply to be fully who you are in this moment, as you are. And to let that be OK for now—underscore *for now*. Perhaps the value of meditation lies precisely in this. Maybe we all need to do one thing in our lives simply for its own sake.

But it would not quite be accurate to call meditation a "doing." It is more accurately described as a way of "being." When we understand that "this is it," it allows us to let go of the past and the future and wake up to who we are now, in this moment, and somehow be more at peace with it, even if it is difficult or painful. Why? Because it is already just like this. It is already as it is. We do have some leverage here, some degrees of freedom in how we are in relationship to the actual, even if it is unpleasant, or lonely, or scary, or worse. And we certainly have agency when it comes to taking action of one kind or another, particularly wise action, which sometimes looks like nothing, as you will see. Accepting that things are as they are is a form of intelligence. It has nothing to do with surrender, passive resignation, or despair. The awareness that holds the unwanted, the unpleasant, the difficult, even the terrifying and the heart-rending, affords us a new degree of freedom to be in wise relationship with the actual. Awareness is intrinsically both a refuge and a source of strength and sanity, of wisdom and compassion, including an honest compassion for ourselves as sometimes frail, vulnerable, and wounded creatures.

People usually don't get this right away. They want to meditate in order to get somewhere else, have a pleasant result, relax, experience a special state, become a better person, reduce or get beyond some source of stress or pain, break out of old habits and patterns, become free or enlightened. All valid reasons to take up meditation practice, but all equally fraught with problems if you expect those things to happen just because now you are meditating. You'll get caught up in wanting to have a "special experience" or in looking for signs of progress, and if you don't feel something special pretty quickly, you may start to doubt the path you have chosen or to wonder whether you are "doing it right."

In most domains of learning, this is only reasonable. Of course you have to see progress sooner or later to keep at something. But meditation is different. From the perspective of meditation, every state is a special state, every moment a special moment.

When we let go of wanting something else to happen in this moment, we are taking a profound step toward being able to encounter what is here now. If we hope to go anywhere or develop ourselves in any way, we can only step from where we are standing. If we don't really know where we are standing—a not-merely-conceptual knowing that comes directly from the cultivation of mindfulness—we may only go in circles, for all our efforts and expectations. So, in meditation practice, the best way to get somewhere is to let go of trying to get anywhere at all.

*

If your mind isn't clouded by unnecessary things,
This is the best season of your life.

WU-MEN

TRY: Reminding yourself from time to time: "This is it." See if there is anything at all that it cannot be applied to. Remind yourself that acceptance of the present moment as it is rather than as you might want it to be has nothing to do with passive resignation in the face of what is happening. It simply means a clear recognition and acknowledgment that *what is happening is happening, and what has happened has already happened.* Acceptance doesn't tell you what to do. What happens next, what you choose to do, has to come out of your understanding of this moment. You might try acting out of a deep knowing of "This is it." Does it influence how you choose to proceed or respond? Is it possible for you to contemplate that in a very real way, *this* may actually be the best season, the best moment of your life? If that was so, what would it mean for you—right now?

Capturing Your Moments

The best way to capture moments is to pay attention. This is how we cultivate mindfulness. Mindfulness means being awake. It means knowing what you are doing and what is going on in your mind. But when we start to focus in on what our own mind is up to, for instance, it is not unusual to quickly go unconscious again, to fall back into an automatic-pilot mode of unawareness. These lapses in awareness are frequently caused by an eddy of dissatisfaction with what we are seeing or feeling in that moment, out of which springs a desire for something to be different, for things to change.

You can easily observe the mind's habit of escaping from the present moment for yourself. Just try to keep your attention focused on any object for even a short period of time. You will find that to cultivate mindfulness, you may have to remember over and over again to be awake and aware. We do this by reminding ourselves to look, to feel, to be, and by bringing the mind back over and over again when it gets lost in thought. It's that simple...checking in from moment to moment, sustaining awareness across a stretch of timeless moments, being here, now...and now...and even, now.

TRY: Asking yourself in this moment, "Am I awake?" "Where is my mind right now?" "And how do I even know that?"

Keeping the Breath in Mind

It helps to have a focus for your attention, an anchor line to tether you to the present moment and to guide you back when the mind wanders. The breath serves this purpose exceedingly well. It can be a true ally. Bringing awareness to our breathing, we remind ourselves that we are here now, so we might as well be fully awake for whatever is already unfolding.

Our breathing can help us in recognizing and inhabiting our moments. It's surprising that more people don't know about this. After all, the breath is always here, right under our noses. You would think just by chance we might have come across its usefulness at one point or another. We even have the phrase "I didn't have a moment to breathe" (or "to catch my breath") to give us a hint that moments and breathing might be connected in an interesting way.

To use your breathing to nurture mindfulness, just tune in to the breath sensations themselves...the feeling of this breath coming into your body and the feeling of this breath leaving your body. That's all. Just feeling the breath and knowing that you're breathing. It doesn't mean deep breathing or forcing your breath, or trying to feel something special, or wondering whether you're doing it right. It doesn't mean thinking about your breathing, either. It's just a bare-bones awareness of *this* breath moving in and *this* breath moving out.

It doesn't have to be for a long time at any one stretch. Using the breath to bring us back to the present moment takes no time at all, only a shift in attention. But great adventures await if you give yourself a little time by the clock to string moments of awareness together, breath by breath and moment by moment.

TRY: Staying with one full inbreath as it comes in, one full outbreath as it goes out, keeping your mind open and free for just this moment, just this breath. Abandon all ideas of getting somewhere or having anything special happen. Just keep returning to the sensations associated with the breath when the mind wanders, stringing moments of mindfulness together, breath by breath by breath. You might try it every once in a while as you read this book.

*

Kabir says: Student, tell me, what is God?
He is the breath inside the breath.

KABIR

Practice, Practice, Practice

It helps to keep at it. As you begin befriending your breath, you see immediately that unawareness is everywhere. Your breath teaches you that not only does unawareness go with the territory; it *is* the territory. It does this by showing you, over and over again, that it's not so easy to stay with the feeling of the breath moving in and out of the body even if you want to. Lots of things intrude, carry us off, prevent us from concentrating. We see that the mind has gotten cluttered over the years, like an attic, filled with old boxes and bags and accumulated junk. Just knowing this is a big step in the right direction.

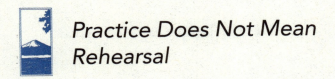

Practice Does Not Mean Rehearsal

We use the word "practice" to describe the cultivation of mindfulness, but it is not meant in the usual sense of a repetitive rehearsing to get better and better so that a performance or a competition will go as well as possible.

Mindfulness practice means that we commit fully in each moment to being present. There is no "performance." There is only this moment. We are not trying to improve ourselves or to get somewhere else. We are not even running after special insights or visions. Nor are we forcing ourselves to be non-judgmental, calm, or relaxed. And we are certainly not promoting self-consciousness, self-centeredness, or ruminations on what is wrong with you or missing from your life. Rather, we are simply inviting ourselves to interface with this moment as best we can in full awareness, with things exactly as they are, with the intention to uncover, discover, or recover a sense of intrinsic calm, wakefulness, clarity, and equanimity already underlying our experience right here and right now.

Of course, with continued practice and the right kind of firm yet gentle effort, a sense of calm and wakefulness, clarity and equanimity develop and deepen on their own, out of your commitment to dwell in stillness and to observe without reacting and without judging (while recognizing that there will be plenty of reacting and judging going on, and that we don't have to compound matters by reacting to or judging any of that second-order activity). Realizations and insights, profound experiences of stillness and joy do come. But it would be incorrect to say that we are practicing to make these experiences happen or that having more of them is better than having fewer of them.

The spirit of mindfulness is to practice for its own sake and just to take each moment as it comes—pleasant or unpleasant, good, bad, or ugly—and then welcome and work with whatever arises because it is what is present now. With this attitude, life itself becomes practice. Then, rather than you doing the meditation practice, it might be more accurate to say that the practice is doing you, and that life itself is serving as your best meditation teacher and guide.

You Don't Have to Go Out of Your Way to Practice

Henry David Thoreau's two years at Walden Pond were above all a personal experiment in mindfulness. He chose to put his life on the line in order to revel in the wonder and simplicity of present moments. But you don't have to go out of your way or find someplace special to practice mindfulness. It is sufficient to make a little time in your life for stillness and what we call non-doing and then simply tune in to your breathing.

All of Walden Pond is right here within your breath. The miracle of the changing seasons is right here, in this moment, within the breath; your parents and your children, your grandchildren and your friends are all here within the breath; your shortcomings and your triumphs are within the breath; the entirety of your body and your mind are within the breath. The breath is the current connecting body and mind, connecting us with everything, connecting our body with the outer world's body. The breath sensations are the current of life streaming through us. There are nothing but golden fish in this stream. All we need to apprehend them clearly is the lens of awareness. We are always in possession of that lens. But it is left to us to make use of it.

*

Time is but the stream I go a-fishing in. I drink at it; but while I drink, I see the sandy bottom and detect how shallow it is. Its thin current slides away, but eternity remains. I would drink deeper; fish in the sky, whose bottom is pebbly with stars.

THOREAU, *Walden*

*

In eternity there is indeed something true and sublime. But all these times and places and occasions are now and here. God himself culminates in the present moment, and will never be more divine in the lapse of all the ages.

THOREAU, *Walden*

Waking Up

Taking up a formal meditation practice by making some time for it each day doesn't mean that you won't be able to think anymore, or that you can't run around and get things done. It means that you are more likely to know what you are doing because you stopped for a while and watched, listened, understood.

Thoreau saw this ever so clearly at Walden Pond. His closing message: "Only that day dawns to which we are awake." If we are to grasp the reality of our life while we have it to live, we will need to wake up to our moments. Otherwise, whole days, even a whole life, could slip past unnoticed, uninhabited, unrealized.

One practical way to do this is to look at other people on occasion and ask yourself whether you are really seeing them or just your thoughts about them. Sometimes our thoughts and opinions act like dream glasses. When we have them on, we see dream children, dream husband, dream wife, dream partner, dream job, dream colleagues, dream friends. We can live in a dream present for a dream future. Without knowing it, we are coloring everything, putting our spin on it all. Although things in the dream may change and give the illusion of being vivid and real, it is still a dream we are caught in. But if we take off the glasses, maybe, just maybe, we might see a little more accurately what is actually unfolding right here, right now, and engage with an extra dose of embodied presence and agency.

Thoreau felt the need to go off on a solitary retreat for an extended period of time (he stayed two years and two months at Walden Pond) to do this. He famously said, "I went to the woods because I wished to live deliberately, to front only the essential facts of life, and see if I could not learn what it had to teach, and not, when I came to die, discover that I had not lived."

His deepest conviction: "To affect the quality of the day, that is the highest of arts.... I have never yet met a man who was quite awake. How could I have looked him in the face?"

TRY: Asking yourself from time to time, "Am I awake now?"

*

My inside, listen to me, the greatest spirit,

the Teacher, is near,

wake up, wake up!

Run to his feet—

he is standing close to your head right now.

You have slept for millions and millions of years.

Why not wake up this morning?

KABIR

Keeping It Simple

If you do decide to start meditating, there's no need to tell other people about it, or talk about why you are doing it or what it's doing for you. In fact, there is no better way to waste your nascent energy and enthusiasm for practice and thwart your efforts so they will be unable to gather momentum. Best to meditate without advertising it.

Every time you get a strong impulse to talk about meditation and how wonderful it is, or how hard it is, or what it's doing for you these days, or what it's not, or you want to convince someone else how wonderful it would be for them, just look at it as more think-ing and go meditate some more. The impulse will pass and every-body will be better off—especially you. This is all the more the case in an era of pervasive social media. Some things are best kept to yourself, especially in their nascent stages, say the first twenty or thirty years.

You Can't Stop the Waves but You Can Learn to Surf

It is a commonly held view that meditation is a way to shut off or shut out the pressures of the world or of your own mind plaguing you. But this is not an accurate impression. Meditation is neither shutting things out nor shutting them off. It is seeing things clearly and deliberately positioning yourself differently in relationship to them.

People who come to the MBSR program at the hospital quickly learn that stress is an inevitable part of life. Although it is true that we can learn, by making intelligent choices, not to make things worse for ourselves in certain ways, there are many things in life over which we have little or no control. Stress is part of life, part of being human, intrinsic to the human condition itself. But that does not mean that we have to be victims in the face of forces large and small in our lives, difficult and rending as they may sometimes be. Believe it or not, it is possible to learn to turn toward them intentionally, to befriend them, work with them, understand them, find meaning in them, make critical choices, and use their energies to grow in strength, wisdom, and compassion. A willingness to embrace and work with what is lies at the core of all meditation practice.

One way to envision how mindfulness works is to think of your mind as the surface of a lake or of the ocean. There are always waves on the water. Sometimes they are big, sometimes they are small, and sometimes they are almost imperceptible. The water's waves are churned up by atmospheric conditions, by winds that come and go and vary in direction and intensity, just as do the winds of stress and change that blow in our lives and stir up waves in our minds.

It is not uncommon for people who aren't familiar with meditation to assume that it involves some kind of special inner manipulation that will magically dampen their amplitude, or suppress them completely, so that the mind's surface will be flat, still, tranquil. But just as you can't put a plexiglass plate on the ocean to attenuate the waves, so you can't artificially suppress the waves of your mind in the service of calmness, and it is not too smart to try. It will only create more tension and inner struggle, not calmness. That doesn't mean that calmness is unattainable. It's just that it cannot be attained by misguided attempts to suppress the mind's natural activity.

It is possible through meditation to find shelter, or you might say, take refuge, from the force of the winds and weather patterns that so frequently agitate the mind. Over time, a good deal of the turbulence may die down from lack of continuous feeding. But ultimately the winds of life and of the mind will blow, do what we may. Meditation is about knowing something about this territory and how to be in wise relationship to it.

The spirit of mindfulness practice was nicely captured many years ago in a poster of a seventy-ish yogi, Swami Satchidananda, in full white beard and flowing robes atop a surfboard riding the waves off a Hawaiian beach. The caption read: "You can't stop the waves, but you can learn to surf."

Thirty years after I quoted him in the first edition of this book, that aphorism is frequently attributed to me. A 2022 Google search showed almost six million instances of my saying it, even though I was quoting someone else. So much for source accuracy in the digital universe.

Can Anybody Meditate?

I get asked this question a lot. I suspect people ask because they think that probably everybody else can meditate except for them. Perhaps they want to be reassured that they are not alone, that there are at least some other people they can identify with, those hapless souls who were born incapable of meditating. But it isn't so simple, and it simply isn't so.

Thinking you are unable to meditate is a little like thinking you are unable to breathe or to focus or relax. Most of us are blessed with being able to breathe effortlessly most of the time. So effortlessly that we tend to take the miracle of effortless breathing for granted. And under the right circumstances, pretty much anybody can focus, anybody can relax. But it does take some degree of training to stabilize these innate capacities and make them readily available. Adopting a formal and regular meditation practice is a form of training the mind itself. In fact, in some traditions, it is called *mind training*. You might also say it is a way of befriending the mind, familiarizing yourself with its habits and energies. You could also think of it as *taming* the mind. And in this day and age, what with apps and YouTube videos, you can certainly engage with disciplined daily practice on your own, as now millions of people are doing to support their glide path into sustained practice.

People often confuse meditation with relaxation or some other special state that you have to get to or feel. When once or twice you try and you don't get anywhere or you didn't feel anything special, then you think you are one of those people who can't meditate.

But meditation is not about feeling a certain way. It's about feeling the way you feel and knowing it in awareness in that moment. It's not about making the mind empty or still, although stillness does deepen in meditation and can be cultivated systematically. Above all, meditation is about letting the mind be as it is and knowing something about *how* it is in this moment. It's not about getting somewhere else or pursuing some special singular "mindfulness state," which doesn't exist, but about allowing yourself to be where and as you already are and letting that be enough for now (again, all puns intended). If you don't understand this, you will think you are constitutionally incapable of meditating. But that itself is just more thinking, and sorely misinformed thinking at that.

True, engaging in the regular formal practice of meditation does require a certain degree of energy and a commitment to stick with it. But then, wouldn't it be more accurate to say, "I won't stick with it," rather than, "I can't do it"? Anybody can sit down and watch their breath or watch their mind. And you don't have to be sitting. You could do it walking, standing, lying down, standing on one leg, running, or taking a bath. But to stay at it for even five minutes requires intentionality. To make it part of your life requires some degree of discipline. So when people say they can't meditate, what they really mean is that they won't make time for it, or that when they try, they don't like what happens and feel thwarted. It isn't what they are looking for or hoping for. It doesn't fulfill their expectations. So maybe they should try again, this time letting go of all the expectations, and just paying attention to whatever is unfolding in the space of awareness, without judging any of it at all.

In Praise of Non-Doing

If you sit down to meditate, even for a moment, it will be a time for non-doing. It is very important not to think that this non-doing is synonymous with doing nothing. They couldn't be more different. Consciousness and intentionality matter here. In fact, they are key.

On the surface, it seems as if there might be two kinds of non-doing, one involving not doing any outward work, the other involving what we might call effortless activity. Ultimately, we come to see that they are the same. It is the inward experience that counts here. What we frequently call formal meditation involves purposefully making a time for stopping all outward activity and cultivating stillness, with no agenda other than being fully present in each moment. Not doing anything. Perhaps such moments of non-doing are the greatest gift one can give oneself.

Thoreau would often sit in his doorway for hours and just watch, just listen, as the sun moved across the sky and the light and shadows changed imperceptibly.

*

There were times when I could not afford to sacrifice the bloom of the present moment to any work, whether of the head or hand. I love a broad margin to my life. Sometimes, in a summer morning, having taken my accustomed bath, I sat in my sunny doorway from sunrise till noon, rapt in a revery, amidst the pines and hickories and sumachs, in undisturbed solitude and stillness, while the birds sang around or flitted noiseless through the house, until by the sun falling in at my west window, or the noise of some traveller's wagon on the distant highway, I was reminded of the lapse of time. I grew in those seasons like corn in the night, and they were far better than any work of the hands would have been. They were not time subtracted from my life, but so much over and above my usual allowance. I realized what the Orientals mean by contemplation and the forsaking of works. For the most part, I minded not how the hours went. The day advanced as if to light some work of mine; it was morning, and lo, now it is evening, and nothing memorable is accomplished. Instead of singing, like the birds, I silently smiled at my incessant good fortune. As the sparrow had its trill, sitting on the hickory before my door, so I had my chuckle or suppressed warble which he might hear out of my nest.

THOREAU, Walden

TRY: Recognizing the bloom of the present moment in your life, in any and maybe even every moment, and in your daily meditation practice if you have one. If you are up early in the morning, go outside if you can and look (a sustained, mindful, attentive looking) at the stars, at the moon, at the clouds, at the dawning light when it comes. Feel the air, the cold, the warmth (a sustained, mindful, attentive feeling). Realize that the world around you is sleeping. Remember that, when you see the stars, you are looking back in time, in some cases millions of years. The past is present now and here.

Then go and sit, or meditate lying down. Let this or any time you practice be your time for you, for letting go of all doing, for shifting into the being mode, in which you simply take up residency in awareness itself, mindfully dwelling in stillness, attending to the moment-to-moment unfolding of the present, adding nothing, subtracting nothing, affirming that "this is it."

The Non-Doing Paradox

The flavor and the sheer joy of non-doing are difficult for Americans to grasp because our culture places so much value on doing, on getting things done, on getting ahead, on progress. Even our leisure tends to be busy and often mindless. The joy of non-doing is that nothing else needs to happen for this moment to be complete. The wisdom in it and the equanimity that comes out of it lie in knowing that something else surely will.

When Thoreau says, "it was morning, and lo, now it is evening, and nothing memorable is accomplished," this is waving a red flag in front of a bull for go-getter, progress-oriented people. But who is to say that his realizations of one morning spent in his doorway are less memorable or have less merit than a lifetime of busyness, lived with scant appreciation for stillness and the bloom of the present moment?

Thoreau was singing a song that needed hearing then as it certainly does now even more. To this day, he is continually pointing out for anyone willing to listen the deep importance of contemplative practice and of nonattachment to any result other than the sheer enjoyment of being, all "far better than any work of the hands would have been." This view recalls the old Zen master who said, "Ho ho. For forty years I have been selling water by the river and my efforts are totally without merit."

It reeks of paradox. The only way you can do anything of value is to have the effort come out of non-doing, and to let go of caring whether it will be of use or not. Otherwise, self-involvement and greediness can sneak in and distort your relationship to the work, or the work itself, so that it is off in some way, biased, tainted, and ultimately not completely satisfying, even if it has merit. Great scientists know this mind state and guard against it because it inhibits the creative process and distorts one's ability to see hitherto unseen connections clearly, which we sometimes call breakthrough insights, or breakthrough moments, none of which can be forced.

Non-Doing in Action

Non-doing can arise within action as well as in stillness. The inward stillness of the doer merges with the outward activity to such an extent that the action does itself. Effortless activity. Nothing is forced. There is no exertion of the will, no small-minded "I," "me," or "mine" to lay claim to a doer or a result, yet nothing is left undone. Non-doing is a cornerstone of mastery in any realm of activity. Here's a classic statement of it from third-century China:

Prince Wen Hui's cook
Was cutting up an ox.
Out went a hand,
Down went a shoulder,
He planted a foot,
He pressed with a knee,
The ox fell apart
With a whisper,
The bright cleaver murmured
Like a gentle wind.
Rhythm! Timing!
Like a sacred dance,
Like "The Mulberry Grove,"
Like ancient harmonies!
"Good work!" the Prince exclaimed,

"Your method is faultless!"
"Method?" said the cook
Laying aside his cleaver,
"What I follow is Tao
Beyond all methods!

"When I first began
To cut up oxen
I would see before me
The whole ox
All in one mass.
After three years
I no longer saw this mass.
I saw the distinctions.

"But now I see nothing
With the eye. My whole being
Apprehends.
My senses are idle. The spirit
Free to work without plan
Follows its own instinct
Guided by natural line,
By the secret opening, the hidden space,
My cleaver finds its own way.
I cut through no joint, chop no bone.

*

"There are spaces in the joints;
The blade is thin and keen:
When this thinness
Finds that space
There is all the room you need!
It goes like a breeze!
Hence I have this cleaver nineteen years
As if newly sharpened!

"True, there are sometimes
Tough joints. I feel them coming,
I slow down, I watch closely,
Hold back, barely move the blade,
And whump! the part falls away
Landing like a clod of earth.

"Then I withdraw the blade,
I stand still
And let the joy of the work
Sink in.
I clean the blade
And put it away."

Prince Wen Hui said,
"This is it! My cook has shown me
How I ought to live
My own life!"

CHUANG TZU

Doing Non-Doing

Non-doing has nothing to do with being indolent or passive. Quite the contrary. It takes great courage and energy to cultivate non-doing, both in stillness and in activity. Nor is it easy to make a special time for non-doing and to keep at it in a disciplined way in the face of everything in our lives that needs to get done, to say nothing of all the distractions at our fingertips and in our earbuds, unless we take them out.

But non-doing doesn't have to be threatening to people who feel they always have to get things done. They might find they get even more "done," and done better, by practicing non-doing. Non-doing simply means letting things be and allowing them to unfold in their own way. Enormous effort can be involved, but it is a graceful, knowledgeable, effortless effort, a "doerless doing" cultivated over a lifetime.

Effortless activity happens at moments in dance and in sports at the highest levels of performance; when it does, it takes everybody's breath away. But it also happens in every area of human activity, from painting to car repair to parenting. Years of practice and experience combine on some occasions, giving rise to a new capacity to let execution unfold beyond technique, beyond exertion, beyond thinking. Action then becomes a pure expression of art, of being, of letting go of all doing—a merging of mind and body in motion. We thrill in watching a superb performance, whether athletic or artistic, because it allows us to participate in the jaw-dropping magic of true mastery, to be uplifted, if only briefly, and perhaps to share in the aspiration that each of us, in our own way, might touch such moments of grace and harmony in the living of our own lives.

Thoreau said, "To affect the quality of the day, that is the highest of arts." The great Martha Graham, speaking of the art of dance, put it this way: "All that is important is this one moment in movement. Make the moment vital and worth living. Do not let it slip away unnoticed and unused."

No meditation master could have spoken truer. We can apprentice ourselves to this work, knowing full well that non-doing is both the work of a lifetime and of no time at all, and conscious all the while that the doing mode is usually so strong in us that, ironically, the cultivating of non-doing takes considerable effort.

Mindfulness meditation is synonymous with the practice of non-doing. We aren't practicing to make things perfect or to do things perfectly. Rather, we practice to grasp and realize (i.e., make real for ourselves) the fact that things already are perfect, perfectly what they are. This has everything to do with holding the present moment in its fullness without imposing anything extra on it, perceiving its purity and the freshness of its potential to give rise to the next moment. Then, knowing what is what, seeing as clearly as possible, and conscious of not knowing more than we actually do, we act, make a move, take a stand, take a chance. Some people speak of this as flow, one moment flowing seamlessly, effortlessly into the next, cradled in the streamed of mindfulness.

TRY: During the day, see whether you can detect the bloom of the present moment in every moment, the ordinary ones, the "in-between" ones, even the hard ones. Work at allowing more things to unfold in your life without forcing them to happen and without rejecting the ones that don't fit your idea of what "should" be happening. See whether you can sense the "spaces" through which you might move with no effort, in the spirit of Chuang Tzu's cook. Notice how, if you can make some time early in the day for being, with no agenda other than to "fall awake," it can change the quality of the rest of your day. Put differently, you might explore whether it doesn't help to *tune* your instrument of being before taking it out on the road, to get a mindful jump on the whole day and thus, potentially and potently, become more capable of recognizing, living inside of, appreciating, and responding to the bloom of each moment.

Patience

Certain attitudes or mental qualities support meditation practice and provide a rich soil in which the seeds of mindfulness can flourish. By purposefully cultivating these qualities, we are actually tilling the soil of our own mind and ensuring that it can serve as a source of clarity, compassion, and right action in our lives.

These inner qualities that support meditation practice cannot be imposed, legislated, or decreed. They can only be cultivated, and this only when you have reached the point where your inner motivation is strong enough to want to cease contributing to your own suffering and confusion and perhaps to that of others. It amounts to behaving ethically—a sorely maligned concept in many circles.

On the radio, I heard someone define ethics as "obedience to the unenforceable." Not bad. You do it for inner reasons, not because someone is keeping score or because you might be punished if you break the rules and get caught. You are marching to the beat of your own drummer. It is an inner hearing you are attending to, just as it is an inner soil that is being tilled for the cultivation of mindfulness. You cannot have either inner or outer harmony without a commitment to ethical behavior. It's the fence that keeps out the goats that will eat all the young shoots in your garden and in the process, if you are not careful, destroy your integrity as well.

I see patience as one of these fundamental ethical attitudes. If you cultivate patience or forbearance on a regular basis, inwardly and outwardly, you almost can't help cultivating mindfulness, and your meditation practice will gradually become richer and more mature. After all, if you really aren't trying to get anywhere else in this moment, patience takes care of itself. It is a remembering that things unfold in their own time. The seasons cannot be hurried. Spring comes, the grass grows by itself. Being in a hurry usually doesn't help, and it can create a great deal of suffering—sometimes in us, sometimes in those who have to be around us.

Patience is an ever-present alternative, even antidote, to the mind's endemic restlessness and impatience. Scratch the surface of impatience, and what you will find lying beneath it, subtly or not so subtly, is anger. It's the strong energy of not wanting things to be the way they are and blaming someone (often yourself) or something for it. This doesn't mean you can't hurry when you have to. It is possible even to hurry patiently, mindfully, moving fast because you have chosen to, because there is a need for it.

From the perspective of patience, things happen because other things happen. Nothing is separate and isolated. There is no absolute, end-of-the-line, the-buck-stops-here root cause for an event. If someone hits you with a stick, you don't get angry at the stick or at the arm that swung it; you get angry at the person attached to the arm. But if you look a little deeper, you can't find a satisfactory root cause or place for your anger even in the person, who literally doesn't know what they are doing and is therefore out of their mind at that moment. Where should the blame lie, or the punishment? Maybe we should be angry at the person's parents for the abuse they may have showered on a defenseless child. Or maybe at the world for its lack of compassion. But what is the world? Are you not a part of that world? Do not you yourself have angry feelings at times, and under some conditions, find yourself in touch with violent, even murderous impulses?

The Dalai Lama evinces no anger toward the Chinese, even though the policy of the Chinese government for more than half a century has been, arguably, to practice genocide toward Tibetans; a form of culturicide toward their institutions, beliefs, and everything they hold dear; and geocide toward the very land they live on. When asked about his apparent lack of anger toward the Chinese by an incredulous reporter at the time he won the Nobel Peace Prize in 1989, the Dalai Lama replied something to the effect that "they have taken everything from us; should I let them take my heart as well?"

This attitude is itself a remarkable display of wisdom, forbearance, and equanimity...the inner peace of knowing what is most fundamental, and the outer peace of embodying that wisdom in one's carriage and action. Peace, and a willingness to be patient in the face of such enormous provocation and suffering, can only come about through the inner cultivation of compassion, a compassion that is not limited to friends but is felt equally for those who, out of ignorance—often seen as evil—may cause you and those you love to suffer.

That degree of selfless compassion is based on what in Buddhism is called "right mindfulness" and "right understanding." It doesn't just spring up spontaneously. It needs to be cultivated, nurtured systematically, practiced. It's not that feelings of anger don't arise. It's that the anger can be used, worked with, metabolized, transmuted, and harnessed so that its energies can nourish patience, compassion, harmony, and wisdom in ourselves and perhaps in others as well.

In taking up the regular discipline of formal meditation practice, we are cultivating the quality of patience every time we stop all the outer activity and drop in on our momentary experience, such as when we take our seat and become aware of the flow of our own breathing. And this invitation to ourselves to be more open, more in touch, more patient with our moments naturally extends itself to other times in our lives as well. We know that things unfold according to their own nature. We can remind ourselves to let our lives unfold in the same way. We don't have to let our anxieties and our desire for certain results dominate the quality of the moment, even when things are painful. When we have to push, we push. When we have to pull, we pull. But we know when not to push too and when not to pull.

Through it all, we attempt to bring balance to the present moment, understanding that in patience lies wisdom, knowing that what will come next will be determined in large measure by how we are now. This is helpful to keep in mind when we get impatient in our meditation practice or when we get frustrated, impatient, or angry in our lives.

*

Do you have the patience to wait

till your mud settles and the water is clear?

Can you remain unmoving

till the right action arises by itself?

LAO-TZU, *Tao-te-Ching*

*

I exist as I am, that is enough,

If no other in the world be aware I sit content,

And if each and all be aware I sit content.

One world is aware, and by far the largest to me, and that is
myself,

And whether I come to my own today or in ten thousand or ten
million years,

I can cheerfully take it now, or with equal cheerfulness, I can
wait.

WALT WHITMAN, *Leaves of Grass*

TRY: Investigating impatience and anger with kindness and genuine interest when they arise. See whether you can adopt a different perspective, one that sees things as unfolding in their own time.
This is especially useful when you are feeling under pressure and

blocked or stymied in something you want or need to do. Hard as it may seem, try not to push the river in that moment but listen carefully to it instead. What does it tell you? What is it telling you to do? If nothing, then just breathe, let things be as they are, let go into patience, continue listening, resting in awareness. If the river tells you something, then do it, but do it mindfully. Then pause, wait patiently, listen again.

As you attend the gentle flow of your own breathing during times of formal meditation practice, notice the occasional pull of the mind to get on to something else, to want to fill up your time or change what is happening. Instead of losing yourself at these times, try to sit patiently with the breath in the body and with a keen awareness of what is unfolding in each moment, allowing it to unfold as it will, without imposing anything on it...just watching, just breathing...embodying stillness, becoming patience.

Letting Go

The phrase "letting go" has to be high in the running for New Age cliché of the last half of the twentieth century. And to this day, it is still overused, abused daily. Yet it is such a powerful inward maneuver that it merits looking into, cliché or not. There is something vitally important to be learned from the practice of letting go.

Letting go means just what it says. It's an invitation to cease clinging to anything—whether it be an idea, a thing, an event, a particular time, or view, or desire. It is a conscious decision to release with full acceptance into the stream of present moments as they are unfolding. To let go means to give up coercing, resisting, or struggling, in exchange for something more powerful and wholesome that comes out of allowing things to be as they are without getting caught up in your attraction to or rejection of them, in the intrinsic stickiness of wanting, of liking and disliking, of the impulse to grasp on to and cling to desires or aversions of all kinds when they arise in the mind. The gesture of letting go is akin to letting your palm open to unhand something you have been holding on to.

But it's not only the stickiness of our desires and aversions concerning outer events that catches us. Nor is it only a holding on with our hands. We hold on even more with our minds, with our strong desire for things to be as we want them to be. We hold on by taking things very personally, even when there is nothing personal about them. We imprison ourselves, get stuck ourselves, by holding—often stubbornly—to narrow and unexamined views, to self-serving and small-minded hopes and wishes. Remembering that it is possible to let go in that very moment invites us to become a bit more transparent to the strong pull of our own likes and dislikes, our oft-unexamined desires and views, and of the persistent opacity of unawareness that drives us to identify with our thoughts and emotions and cling to them regardless of their validity or toxicity. To be transparent requires that we allow fears and insecurities to play themselves out in the welcoming, open-hearted embrace of full awareness.

Letting go is only possible if we can bring awareness and acceptance to the nitty-gritty of just how stuck we can get, and if we can, give ourselves permission to recognize the lenses we slip so unconsciously between observer and observed that then filter and color, bend and shape our view. We are capable of opening in those sticky moments—especially if we are able to capture them in awareness and recognize when we are getting caught up in either pursuing and clinging or in condemning and rejecting in seeking our own gain—and simply issuing a friendly restraining order to ourselves in that moment.

Stillness, insight, and wisdom arise only when we can give ourselves permission to settle into being complete in this moment, as we are, without having to seek or hold on to or reject anything. This is a testable proposition. Try it out just for fun. See for yourself whether letting go when a part of you really wants to hold on doesn't bring a deeper satisfaction than clinging.

Non-Judging Invites Discernment

It doesn't take long in meditation to discover that part of our mind is constantly evaluating our experiences, comparing them with other experiences or holding them up against expectations and standards that we ourselves create, often out of fear. Fear that I'm not good enough, that bad things will happen, that good things won't last, that other people might hurt me, that I won't get my way, that only I know anything, that I'm the only one who doesn't know anything. We tend to see things through tinted glasses: through the lens of whether something is good for me or bad for me, or whether or not it conforms to my beliefs or philosophy. If it is good in that sense, I like it. If it is bad, I don't like it. If it is neither, I have no feelings about it one way or the other and may hardly notice it at all. But negatively valenced emotional content often seems to be accorded more salience by the brain than even significantly positive experiences. Technically speaking, this is an evolutionary inheritance of sorts, a so-called negativity bias that has kept humans alive for hundreds of thousands of years and more. It serves its purpose at times, no doubt, even today. But mindfulness applied in such moments can help us to recognize and modulate that inbuilt tendency in some pretty important and life-affirming ways.

When you drop in to a period of formal meditation practice and attempt, even for a relatively brief time, to dwell in stillness, the judging mind can come through like a relentless foghorn. *I can't take this pain in my knee.... This is boring.... I like this feeling of stillness.... I had a good meditation yesterday, but today I'm having a bad meditation.... It's not working for me. I'm no good at this. I'm no good, period.* This type of thinking dominates the mind and weighs it down. It's like carrying around a suitcase full of rocks on your head. It feels good to put it down. Imagine how it might feel to suspend all your habitual judging and instead let each moment be just as it is, without attempting to evaluate it as "good" or "bad" from such a self-preoccupied and exclusively self-centered perspective. This gesture alone might afford a momentary taste of stillness, of liberation. You would be immediately at home in your own being, at least for that fleeting timeless moment.

Meditation involves intentionally cultivating a non-judging attitude toward whatever arises in the mind, come what may. But adopting a non-judgmental attitude toward momentary experience doesn't mean judging won't be going on. Of course it will be. It is in the very nature of the mind to compare, to judge and evaluate. When it occurs, we don't try to stop it or ignore it, any more than we would try to stop any other thoughts that might come through our mind.

The tack we take with mindfulness meditation is simply to become aware as best we can of *whatever* is arising in the mind or the body and to recognize it without either condemning it or pursuing it, knowing that our judgments are themselves an intrinsic part of the landscape, natural arisings, like weather patterns in the mind. They invariably take the form of limited and often limiting *thoughts about* experience. In cultivating greater mindfulness, what we are interested in is the direct apprehending of experience itself—whether it is of an inbreath, an outbreath, a sensation or feeling, a sound, an impulse, a thought, a perception, or a judgment—simply recognizing it and holding it in awareness for that moment, which is always *this moment*. And as we practice in this way, we remain attentive to the possibility of getting caught up in judging or even despairing about how judgmental we are, or in labeling some judgments as good and others bad.

While our thinking colors virtually all experience, if we are honest with ourselves we might recognize that, more often than not, our thoughts tend to be less than completely accurate. Usually they are merely uninformed private opinions, reactions, and prejudices based on limited knowledge and influenced primarily by our past conditioning. All the same, when not recognized as such and named, our thinking can undermine our ability to see clearly in the present moment. We get caught up in thinking we know what we are seeing and feeling, and needing, and in reflexively projecting our judgments out onto everything we take in. Just becoming familiar with this deeply entrenched pattern and watching it moment by moment as it arises can lead to greater non-judgmental receptivity, and acceptance, to say nothing of insight into how easy it is to undermine our own sovereignty.

A non-judging orientation certainly does not mean that you cease knowing how to act or behave responsibly and ethically, or that whatever others do is automatically okay. It simply means that we can act with much greater clarity and authenticity in our own lives, and be more balanced, more effective, and more ethical in our activities, when we are aware that we ourselves are immersed in a stream of mostly unconscious and highly reactive liking and disliking, identifying and disidentifying, which can easily carry us away from recognizing the complex reality of things as they actually are, and which can also carry us away from the intrinsic beauty, wonder, and integrity of our own unique being. Without ongoing awareness, automatic dualistic habits of liking and disliking can more readily take up permanent residence in us, feeding addictive behaviors and habits of one kind or another and clouding the mind.

In this context, it is super-important to differentiate our capacity for judging from another very powerful attribute we also possess and can deploy and refine in our practice, namely our capacity for *discernment*. What develops over time in the cultivation of mindfulness is our ability to look deeply into something and perceive distinctions keenly and with clarity. Discernment is the ability to see this *and* that, as opposed to this *or* that, to see the whole picture, and its fine details, to see gradations, not just binary categories such as black and white, good or bad, us and them in absolute terms. Being discerning is an inward sign of wisdom and respect for reality because we are taking note of subtleties as well as the gross outline of things, aware of complexity and mystery, aware of an intrinsic interconnectedness between opposites. There is an elemental fairness in it, a rightness in it, because it is truer to the whole of reality. "Non-judgmental awareness," as I use the term, describes attending with discernment, again, as best we can in any moment.

When we speak of mindfulness being a non-judgmental aware-ness, it is not an appeal to willful ignorance or vacuousness when it comes to essential distinctions, ethical and otherwise. The term *non-judgmental* doesn't mean that we don't see what is going on because we are refusing to perceive necessary and important dis-tinctions. In fact, it is only through being non-judgmental that it might be possible to see and feel what is actually happening, to see past surface appearances and the filters of our own limited opin-ions, our likes and dislikes, beliefs and fears, our unexamined and sometimes unconscious prejudices, and our deep longing for things to be a certain way. Awareness can hold even our own judging in mind and know it for what it is. The challenge: Can we recognize such ingrained habits of mind when they arise with some degree of compassion and not judge ourselves for being so reflexively judg-mental? In recognizing the significance of what we are seeing, dis-cernment gives rise to wisdom. It frees us to act more wisely in any and all life situations without getting so caught up in our prefer-ences that we can no longer see clearly. It is in the very nature of the mind to fall into binary thinking, liking and disliking. But without the tempering alchemy of discernment, our judgments will tend to be inaccurate, unwise, unconscious, and, ultimately, imprisoning. What is more, they will tend to drive unfortunate actions.

With discernment, we are able to recognize and name the seeds of acquisitiveness or craving, however subtle, when they arise in the mind engaged in pursuing the things or results that we like. With that very same capacity for discernment, we are equally able to rec-ognize the seeds of aversion or hatred in our reflexive maneuvering to avoid or reject the things we don't like. Those moments of recognition and discernment nurtured through ongoing mindfulness practice can reveal to us that such habitual tendencies really are at play in our own minds to one extent or another almost all the time, and that they need to be worked with skillfully if we are going to embody any degree of sanity and wakefulness in our lives. It's no exaggeration to say that those tendencies toward grasping and rejecting carry a chronic, virus-like toxicity that prevents us from seeing things as they actually are and mobilizing our true potential for ongoing learning, growing, healing, and transformation moment by moment by moment across the life span—right up to the moment of death.

Trust

Trust is a feeling of confidence or conviction that things can unfold within a dependable framework that embodies order and integrity. We may not always understand what is happening to us, or to another, or what is occurring in a particular situation; but if we trust ourselves, or another, or we place our trust in a process or an ideal, we can find a powerful stabilizing element embracing security, balance, and openness within the trusting that, in some way, if not based on naiveté, intuitively guides us and protects us from harm or self-destruction.

A robust feeling of trust is important to cultivate in mindfulness practice. For if we do not trust in our ability to observe, to be open and attentive, to reflect upon experience, to learn and to grow from observing and attending, to know something deeply, with a degree of intimacy and conviction based on directly experiencing it, we will hardly persevere in cultivating any of these abilities. They will either lie dormant or wither from lack of nurturance.

Part of mindfulness practice is to cultivate a trusting heart. So it might be good to begin by looking into what we can trust in ourselves. If we don't immediately know what is trustworthy in ourselves, maybe we need to look a little deeper, to dwell a little longer with ourselves in stillness and in simply being. If we are unaware of what we are doing a good deal of the time, and we don't particularly like the way things have been turning out in our lives of late, perhaps it's time to pay closer attention, to be more in touch, to observe the choices we make and their consequences down the road.

Perhaps we could experiment with trusting the present moment a bit more, accepting whatever it is we find ourselves feeling or thinking or seeing precisely *because* it is what is present now. If we can take a stand here—say by intentionally taking our seat in meditation for a stretch of time—even a short stretch by the clock—and let go into the full texture of now, we may find that this very moment, as it is, however it is, is worthy of our trust. From such experiments, conducted over and over again, may come a new sense that some- where deep within us resides a profoundly healthy interior resource—we might call it intrinsic wisdom—that we can tap into and thereby come to see is worthy of our trust.

*

Be strong then, and enter into your own body;

there you have a solid place for your feet.

Think about it carefully!

Don't go off somewhere else!

Kabir says this: just throw away all thoughts of imaginary things,

and stand firm in that which you are.

KABIR

Generosity

Generosity is another quality that, like patience, letting go, non-judging, and trust, provides a solid foundation for mindfulness practice. You might experiment with using the intentional cultivation of generosity as a vehicle for deep self-observation and inquiry as well as an exercise in giving. A good place to start is with yourself. See whether you can give yourself gifts that may be true blessings, such as self-acceptance or some time each day with no purpose. Practice feeling deserving enough to accept these gifts without obligation—to simply receive from yourself, and from the universe. After all, your very life is such a gift, as are the lives of everybody you hold dear.

See if you can be in touch with a dimension of your own being that, like life itself, is rich and intrinsically magnanimous beyond reckoning. Let that dimension radiate its energy outward through the entirety of your body and beyond. Experiment with giving away this energy—in little ways at first—directing it toward yourself and toward others with no thought of gain or return. Give more than you think you can, trusting that you are richer than you think. Celebrate this richness. Give as if you had inexhaustible wealth.

I am not talking solely of money or material possessions, although it can be wonderfully growth-enhancing, uplifting, and truly helpful to share material abundance or other benefits of privilege. Rather, what is being suggested here is that you practice sharing the fullness of your being, your intrinsic beauty, the best of who you are, your enthusiasm, your vitality, your spirit, your trust, your openness—above all, your presence. Share it with yourself, with your family, with the world.

TRY: Noticing any resistance to the impulse to give, the worries about the future, the feeling that you may be giving too much, or the thought that it won't be appreciated "enough," or that you will be exhausted from the effort, or that you won't get anything out of it in return, or that you don't have enough yourself. Consider the possibility that none of these are actually true, that they may simply be forms of inertia, constriction, and fear-based calculations. These thoughts and feelings are the rough edges of self-cherishing and clinging, which rub up against the world and frequently cause us and others pain and a sense of distance, isolation, and diminishment. Giving sands down such rough edges and helps us become more mindful of our intrinsic wealth. By practicing mindfulness of generosity, by giving and by observing its effects on us and others, we are transforming ourselves, shedding to some degree unhelpful and limiting attachments and thereby possibly discovering more authentic and fearless versions of ourselves.

You may protest that you don't have enough energy or enthusiasm or material resources to give anything away, that you are already feeling depleted, overwhelmed, or impoverished. Or you may have the feeling that all you do is give, give, give, and that it is just taken for granted by others, not appreciated or even seen. Or you may come to see that you are using your giving as a way to hide from pain and fear, and as a way of making sure others appreciate you or feel dependent on you. Such difficult patterns and relationships themselves call out for attention, careful scrutiny, and kindness. Mindless giving is never healthy or generous. It is important to understand your motivation for giving and to know when some kinds of giving are not a display of generosity but rather of fear and insecurity.

In the mindful and openhearted cultivation of generosity, it is not necessary to give everything away, or even anything. Above all, generosity is an inward giving, a feeling, a willingness to share your own being with the world. Most important is to trust and honor your instincts but, at the same time, to walk the edge and take some risks as part of your own experimenting along these lines. Perhaps you need to give less or to trust your intuition about exploitation or unhealthy motives or impulses on your part or on the part of others. Perhaps you do need to give, but in a different way, or to different people or causes. Perhaps most of all, you need to give to yourself first for a while. Then you might try giving others a tiny bit more than you think you can, consciously noting and letting go of any ideas of getting anything in return.

Initiate giving. Don't wait for someone to ask. See what happens—especially to you. You may find that you gain a greater clarity about yourself and about your relationships, as well as more energy rather than less. You may find that, rather than exhausting yourself or your resources, you are replenishing both. Such is the power of mindful, selfless generosity. At the deepest level, there is no giver, no gift, and no recipient...only the universe rearranging itself.

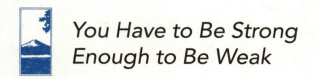

You Have to Be Strong Enough to Be Weak

If you are a strong-willed and accomplished person, you may often give the impression that you are invulnerable to feeling inadequate or insecure or hurt. This can be very isolating and ultimately cause you and others great pain. Other people will be all too happy to take in that impression and to collude in propagating it by projecting a Rock of Gibraltar persona onto you that doesn't allow you to have any real feelings. In fact, you can all too easily drift out of touch with your own true feelings behind an intoxicating shield of image and aura. This isolation happens a lot to fathers in the nuclear family and to people in positions of relative power everywhere.

Thinking of yourself as getting stronger through the meditation practice can create a similar dilemma. You can start believing in and acting out the part of the supremely equanimous, invulnerable, accomplished meditator—the one who has everything under control and is wise enough to deal with everything without being caught up in reactive emotions. In the process, you can cleverly arrest your own development without even knowing it. We all have an emotional life. We wall ourselves off from it at our own peril.

So, when you notice yourself building up an image of invincibility, or strength, or special knowledge, or wisdom based on your meditative experiences, thinking perhaps that you're getting somewhere in your practice, and you start talking a lot about meditation in a way that is self-promotional and inflationary, it's a good idea to bring mindfulness to that mind-set and to ask yourself whether you are running from your vulnerability, or perhaps from grief you may be carrying, or from fear or insecurity of some sort. If you are truly strong, there is little need to emphasize it to yourself or to others. Best to take another tack entirely and direct your attention where you fear most to look. You can do this by allowing yourself to welcome and feel whatever is here to be felt in the body, the mind, and the heart in any given moment; to not have to have so many opinions about everything; to not appear invincible or unfeeling to others but instead to be in touch with and appropriately open about your feelings. What may look like weakness or vulnerability is actually where your strength lies. And what looks like strength can at times be a cover for feelings of acute vulnerability, an attempt to hide your fear from others and maybe even from yourself, ultimately merely a contrivance, an act, a facade, however convincing it might appear to others, or even to yourself.

TRY: Recognizing the ways in which you meet obstacles with immediate harshness. Experiment with being soft when your impulse is to be hard, generous when your impulse is to be withholding, open when your impulse is to close up or shut down emotionally and withdraw. When there is grief or sadness or feelings of inadequacy, try putting out the welcome mat and inviting it all in. Allow yourself to feel whatever you are feeling. Why not? It is already here anyway. Notice any labels you attach to crying or feeling vulnerable. Let go of the labels. Just feel what you are feeling, all the while cultivating moment-to-moment awareness, riding the waves of "up" and "down," "good" and "bad," "weak" and "strong," "worthy" and "unworthy," until you see that they are all inadequate to fully describe your experience. Be with the experience itself. Rest in awareness. Trust in your deepest strength of all: to be present, to be awake.

Voluntary Simplicity

Maybe you experience this as well...the impulse frequently arises in me to squeeze another this or another that into this moment. Just this phone call, or just another email that simply has to be read or responded to, or just stopping off here on my way there. Never mind that it might be in the opposite direction.

I've learned to recognize this impulse to fill up all my moments with doing or distraction and the even stronger impulse to succumb to it. I work hard at saying no to it. It would have me eat breakfast with my eyes riveted on my phone or the newspaper until the breakfast is consumed but not actually tasted or experienced in its moment-by-moment actuality. Any distracter will do: reading for the hundredth time the dietary contents of the cereal box or the amazing free offer from the company. The impulse to self-distract doesn't care what it feeds on, as long as it's feeding. I find the newspaper, especially in analog form, an especially seductive draw, but it could be anything, your favorite social media or app, the news on a screen, a catalog that came in the mail unbidden, or whatever else is around. The craving for distraction scavenges to fill time, conspires with my own mind to keep me unconscious, lulled in a fog of numbness to a certain extent, just enough to fill or overfill my belly while I actually miss the experience of eating breakfast. It has me unavailable to others at those times, missing the play of light on the table, the smells in the room, the energies of the moment.

I like to practice voluntary simplicity to counter such impulses and make sure nourishment comes at a deeper level. It involves intentionally doing only one thing at a time and making sure I am here for it. Many occasions present themselves: taking a walk, for instance. Voluntary simplicity means going fewer places in one day rather than more, seeing less so I can see more, doing less so I can do more, acquiring less so I can have more. It all ties in. Decades ago, it was not an option for me as a father of young children, a breadwinner, a husband, an oldest son to my aging parents, a person who cared and still cares deeply about his work in the world to go off to one Walden Pond or another and sit under a tree for a few years, listening to the grass grow and the seasons change, much as the impulse beckoned then and does now even more, when retreat is much more an option at this stage of life. But within the organized chaos and complexity of family life and work, then and now, with all their demands and responsibilities, frustrations and unsurpassed gifts, the practice of mindfulness recognizes innumerable occasions for choosing simplicity in small but hardly insignificant ways.

Slowing everything down is a big part of this. Telling my mind and body to stay put playing with a grandchild rather than checking my email, not reacting to inner impulses to call or text or email someone right in that moment, choosing not to acquire new things on impulse, not to succumb to clickbait and rabbit holes or to the siren call of devices and now—if one cares to, and a lot of folks do—the looming seductions of chatbots and the metaverse—mindfully demurring to such siren calls moment by moment can be an effective way to simplify life a little. For me, other choices might be just to sit for an evening and do nothing, to read a book, or go for a walk with my wife, to gaze at the moon, or feel the air on my face under the trees, or go to sleep early.

Regarding work, as best I can, I practice saying no to keep my life simple, and I find I never do it enough. It's an arduous discipline all its own and well worth the effort. Yet it is also tricky. There are needs and opportunities to which one must respond. A commitment to voluntary simplicity in the midst of the world on fire is a delicate balancing act. It is always in need of fine-tuning, further inquiry, ongoing attention, and listening to the compelling need for wise engagement and for more and more inclusive activism for the sake of our species and our planet.

The notion of voluntary simplicity also reminds me that in an ecology of mind, body, and world in which everything is interconnected, every moment is a branch point, and every choice carries far-reaching and often unanticipated and unknowable consequences. We don't get to control it all. But voluntarily choosing simplicity whenever possible adds to life an element of deepest freedom that so easily eludes us. It also affords countless opportunities to discover that less may actually be more, much more. Sustainability on planet Earth, if we are to attain it, will very soon require us first-world inhabitants to simplify our personal needs and habit-bound desires, and recognize the until-recently-hidden costs of those desires to the planet's life-sustaining ecosystems. If the need for voluntary simplicity was compelling in Thoreau's time, it is infinitely more compelling in ours. It also provides a pathway out of habits of perpetual self-distraction and absorption we are so easily seduced into now.

Studies show that on average, people check their phones at least several hundred times a day, the young even more. We run the risk of losing our analog being and its inherent genius before we even learn how to inhabit and make use of its full dimensionality. Our minds are the product of billions of years of evolution, of this infinitesimally tiny part of the universe shaping itself into a livable planet, just the right distance from its star to give rise, in the unimaginable reaches of time, to its current life-forms, including you and me, and to the compelling possibility and potential of waking up to the actuality of things. Let's not give up that inheritance.

*

Simplicity, simplicity, simplicity! I say let your affairs be as two or three, and not a hundred or a thousand; instead of a million count half a dozen....In the midst of this chopping sea of civilized life, such are the clouds and storms and quicksands and the thousand-and-one items to be allowed for, that a man has to live, if he would not founder and go to the bottom and not make his port at all, by dead reckoning, and he must be a great calculator indeed who succeeds. Simplify, Simplify.

THOREAU, *Walden*

Concentration

Concentration is a cornerstone of mindfulness practice. Your mindfulness will only be as robust as the capacity of your mind to be calm and stable. Without at least some degree of calmness and stability, both of which develop through ongoing cultivation, it is very difficult to sustain the open presence and clear seeing characteristic of mindfulness.

Concentration can be practiced either hand in hand with mindfulness or separately. You can think of concentration as the capacity of the mind to sustain an unwavering attention on one object of observation. It is cultivated by attending to one thing, such as the breath, and just limiting one's focus to that. In Sanskrit, concentration is called *samadhi*, or "one-pointedness." Samadhi is developed and deepened by continually bringing what is sometimes referred to as the "flashlight of attention" back to the breath every time it wanders off somewhere else, to maximize one-pointedness in the attending. When practicing strictly concentrative forms of meditation, we purposefully refrain from any efforts to inquire into areas such as where the mind went when it wandered off, or that there are subtle or not-so-subtle fluctuations in the quality of each breath. Our energy is directed solely toward experiencing this breath coming in, this breath going out, or some other single object of attention. With extended practice, the mind tends to become better and better at staying on the breath, or noticing even the earliest impulse to become distracted by something else and either resisting its pull in the first place and staying on the breath or quickly returning to it.

With intensive practice, a calmness develops that has a remarkably satisfying quality to it. It is steadfast, profound, hard to disturb, no matter what comes up. It is a great gift to oneself to be able periodically to cultivate samadhi over an extended period of time. This is most readily accomplished on long, silent meditation retreats, when one can withdraw from the world for this very purpose.

The stability and calmness that come with one-pointed concentration practice form the foundation for the cultivation of mindfulness. Without some degree of samadhi, your mindfulness will not be very strong. You can look deeply into something only if you can sustain your looking without being constantly thrown off by distractions or by the agitation of your own mind. The deeper your concentration, the deeper the potential for open presence and for seeing clearly whatever is arising, in other words, for mindfulness.

The experience of deep samadhi is very pleasant. In attending to the breath with one-pointed concentration, everything else falls away—including thoughts, feelings, the outside world. Samadhi is characterized by absorption in stillness and undisturbed peacefulness. A taste of this stillness can be attractive, even intoxicating. One naturally finds oneself seeking the tranquility and simplicity of a condition characterized by absorption and bliss.

But concentration practice, however strong and satisfying, is incomplete without mindfulness to complement and deepen it. By itself, it resembles a withdrawal from the world. Its characteristic energy is closed rather than open, absorbed rather than available, trancelike rather than fully awake. What is missing is the energy of curiosity, inquiry, investigation, openness, availability, and engagement with the full range of phenomena experienced by human beings. This is the domain of mindfulness practice, in which one-pointedness and the ability to bring calmness and stability of mind to the present moment are put in the service of looking deeply into and understanding the interconnectedness of the entire range of life experiences and our place and responsibilities within this web of interconnectivity.

Honing the skill of concentration can be of great value, but it can also be seriously limiting if you get seduced by the pleasant quality of this inner experience and use it as a subtle or not-so-subtle way to escape from life in a complex and very challenged world. You might be tempted to eschew the messiness of daily living and complex relationships for the tranquility of solitude, stillness, and peacefulness. This of course would be an attachment to stillness, and like any strong attachment, it is a form of clinging that can easily lead to self-centeredness, an ignoring of important but unrecognized dimensions of reality, and thus, delusion. If not tempered by mindfulness, one-pointedness can arrest development and short-circuit the flourishing of embodied wisdom.

Vision

It is virtually impossible, and senseless anyway, to commit your-self to a daily meditation practice without some view of why you are doing it, what its value might be in your life, a sense of why this might be your way and not just another tilting at imaginary windmills.

In traditional societies, this vision was supplied and continually reinforced by the culture. If you were a Buddhist, you might practice because the whole culture valued meditation as the path to clarity, compassion, and Buddhahood, a path of wisdom leading to the erad-ication of suffering. But in the Western cultural mainstream, until very recently there was precious little support for choosing such a personal path of discipline and constancy, especially such an unusual one involving effort but non-doing, energy but no tangible "prod-uct." What is more, any superficial or romantic notions we might harbor of becoming a better person—more calm or more clear or more compassionate—don't endure for long when we come face-to-face with the pressing demands of our everyday lives, the turbulence of our minds and bodies, and ultimately, the prospect of getting up early in the morning when it is cold and dark to sit by yourself and be in the present moment with no agenda other than to be awake. Without some profound vision or intuition in the very forefront of your mind and deep in your heart about your own potential for waking up and living a more embodied and meaningful life, getting up early to meditate is way too easily put off or seen as trivial or of secondary importance—the mind will invariably conjure up endless rationalizations for why it can always wait while you catch a little more sleep or at least stay warm in bed. Even the accumulated scientific evidence that mindfulness might be profoundly beneficial in numerous ways won't be motivating for all that long.

If you hope to bring meditation into your life in any kind of long-term, committed way—as a Way of being rather than one more thing you are saddling yourself with to do—you will need a sustaining vision that is truly your own, one that is deep and tenacious and that lies close to the core of who and what you believe yourself to be, what you value in your life, and where you see yourself going. Only the strength of such a dynamic vision and the motivation from which it springs can possibly keep you on the path of a consistent meditation practice year in and year out. It entails a willingness to practice formally as best you can on a regular basis, pretty much every day, whether you feel like it or not, bringing mindfulness to bear on whatever is happening, to open to whatever is being experienced in the present moment, letting awareness itself point to where any holding or clinging might be operating, and recognizing that the possibility of letting go and falling wake in any and every moment is always present, if you are.

Meditation practice is hardly romantic. The ways in which we need to grow are usually those we are the most supremely defended against and are least willing to admit even exist, let alone take an undefended, mindful peek at and then act on to change. It won't be sustaining enough to have a quixotic idea of yourself as a meditator or a more mindful person. Nor will it be of much use in the long term to simply believe that meditation will be "good for you" because it has been good for others, or because Eastern wisdom sounds romantic or deep to you, or because you are already in a more or less mechanical habit of "meditating," or even because the scientific evidence of its value at this point in time clearly suggests that this is the case. The vision or motivation we are speaking of has to come from someplace deep inside. It also has to be reaffirmed, rediscovered, and renewed pretty much every day. It has to be right out front in our consciousness all the time, because mindfulness itself requires being in touch with our core motivations, our deepest aspirations, our abiding intentions moment by moment, as well as alert to our capacity for endless self-deception. Otherwise, we might as well stay in bed and get some more sleep.

The practice itself has to become the daily embodiment of your vision and contain what you value most deeply. It doesn't mean trying to change or be different from how you are: calm when you're not feeling calm, or kind when you really feel angry. Rather, it is bearing in mind what is most important to you so that it is not lost or betrayed in the heat and reactivity, nor in the dullness of a particular moment. If mindfulness is deeply important to you, then every moment is an opportunity to practice.

For example, suppose angry feelings come up at some point in your day. If you find yourself feeling angry and expressing it, you will also find yourself monitoring that expression and its effects moment by moment. You may be in touch with its validity as a feeling state, with the antecedent causes of your strong feeling, and the way it is coming out in your body gestures and stances, in your tone of voice, in your choice of words and arguments, as well as the impression it is making on others. There is much to be said for the conscious expression of anger, and it is well-known medically and psychologically that suppressing anger in the sense of internalizing it is unhealthy, particularly if it becomes habitual. But it is also unhealthy to vent anger uncontrollably as a matter of habit and reaction, however "justifiable." You can feel it cloud the mind. It breeds feelings of aggression and violence—even if the anger is in the service of righting a wrong or getting something important to happen—and thus intrinsically warps what is, whether you are in the right or not. You can feel this even when you can't stop yourself sometimes. Mindfulness can put you in touch with the toxicity of the anger to yourself and to others. I always come away from it feeling that there is something inadequate about anger, even when I am objectively on high ground. Its innate toxicity taints all it touches. If its energy can be transmuted to forcefulness and wisdom, without the smoke and fire of self-absorption or self-righteousness, then its power multiplies, and so does its capacity to transform both the object of the anger and the source.

So, if you practice purposefully expanding the context of the anger (yours or someone else's) right in those very moments in which it is arising and peaking, knowing that there must be something larger and more fundamental that you are forgetting in the heat of the emotion, then you can touch an awareness inside yourself that is not attached to or invested in the anger-fire. Awareness itself is not angry. Awareness sees the anger, knows the depth of the anger, and is larger than the anger. It can therefore hold the anger the way a pot contains food. The pot of awareness helps us to cradle and contain the anger and to see that it may be producing more harmful effects than beneficial ones, even if that is not our aim. In this way, it helps us cook the anger, digest the anger, so that we can use it effectively, and, in changing from an automatic *reacting* to a more mindful *responding*, perhaps move beyond it altogether. This and other options stem from a careful listening in the moment to the dictates of the whole situation, when, in Wu-men's words, our mind is not clouded by unnecessary things.

Thus, our vision has to do with our deepest longing, with our values, with our personal blueprint or aspiration for what is most important in life. It is what we enact. It is rooted in first principles. If you believe in love, do you manifest it or just talk a lot? If you believe in compassion, in non-harming, in kindness, in wisdom, in generosity, in calmness, in solitude, in non-doing, in being evenhanded and clear, how do you manifest these qualities in your daily life? This is the level of intentionality required to keep your meditation practice vital, so that it doesn't become a purely mechanical exercise, driven only by the forces of habit, belief, or identity building.

*

Renew thyself completely each day; do it again, and again, and forever again.

CHINESE INSCRIPTION CITED

BY THOREAU IN *Walden*

TRY: Asking yourself why you meditate or why you want to meditate. Don't believe your first answers. Just write down a list of whatever comes to mind. Continue asking yourself. Also, inquire about your values, about what you honor most in life. Make a list of what is really important to you. Ask yourself, What is my vision, my map for where I am and where I am going? Does this vision reflect my true values and intentions? Am I remembering to embody those values? Do I practice living my intentions? Do I walk my talk? How am I right now in my job, in my family, in my relationships, with myself at this particular age and stage of life, and with what is going on in the world? Is there any separation between how I am and how I aspire to be? How might I live/embody my vision, my values? How do I bring them from abstract desires and thoughts in my head into the domain of embodied being, residing in my bones and emanating from my heart? How do I relate to ignorance and suffering, both my own and others'?

Meditation Develops Full Human Beings

I'm told that in Pali, the original language of the Buddha, there is no one word corresponding to our word "meditation," even though meditation arose, evolved, and flourished to an extraordinary degree in ancient Indian culture. One Pali word that is frequently used is *bhavana*, originally an agricultural term meaning cultivation or development. In regard to meditation, bhavana translates as "development through mental training." To me, this strikes the mark; meditation really is about ongoing human development across the life span via the intentional cultivation of innate qualities, such as kindness, equanimity, and insight stemming from the impulse to investigate, to inquire deeply into one's own being and one's relationship with everything else, that is, the nature of reality itself and the nature of the mind that wants to and can ask such questions and investigate effectively in the first place. It is a natural extension of cutting teeth, growing an adult-sized body, working and making things happen in the world, raising a family, going into debt of one kind or another (even if only to yourself through bargains that may feedback in time to imprison heart and soul), and realizing that you too will grow old and die. At some time or another, you are practically forced to sit down and contemplate your life, and question who you are and where the meaning lies in the arc of your life in this moment.

The old fairy tales are ancient maps offering guidance in their own way for the development of full human beings. The wisdom of these tales comes down to our day from a time before writing, having been shared in twilight and darkness around fires for thousands of years. Although they are entertaining and engaging stories in their own right, they are so in large part because they are emblematic of the dramas we might encounter as we grow up and seek wholeness, happiness, and peace. The kings and queens, princes and princesses, dwarfs and witches of those tales are not merely personages "out there." We know them intuitively as aspects of our own psyches, strands of our own being, groping toward fulfillment. We house the ogre and the witch, and they have to be faced and honored, or they will consume us (eat us up). Fairy tales from all cultures and continents are ancient guidance, distilled through millennia of telling, transmitting a wisdom critical to our instinctual survival, growth, and integration as human beings in the face of the inner and outer demons and dragons, dark woods and wastelands of our own inherited and still-operational preindustrial minds and time. These stories remind us that it is indeed very much worth seeking the metaphorical altar where our own fragmented and isolated strands of being can find each other and "marry," bringing new levels of integration, harmony, and understanding to our lives—to the point where we might actually live happily ever after, which really means in the timeless here and now. These ancient stories are wise and surprisingly sophisticated blueprints for the full development of human beings.

One recurrent theme in the fairy stories is that of a young child, usually a prince or a princess, who loses his or her golden ball.

Whether we ourselves are a he or a she or a they, old or young, we each contain both prince and princess (among countless other figures), and there was a time we each radiated with the golden innocence and infinite promise carried by youth. And we still carry that golden radiance, or can recover it, if we take care not to let our development become arrested.

The celebrated poet Robert Bly loved pointing out that between losing the golden ball, which seems to happen first around age eight, and taking any steps to recover it or even to recognize that it has gotten away from us might take thirty or forty years, whereas in fairy tales, which take place "once upon a time" and therefore outside of ordinary time, usually it only takes a day or two. But in both instances a bargain needs to be made first, a bargain with our own suppressed shadow energies, symbolized by a frog or perhaps by a hairy wild man who resides under the pond in the forest, as in the story of Iron John.

Before that bargain can be made, you have to know that these creatures are there inside of us: the prince, the princess, the frog, the wild man, the wild woman, and many more. A willingness to converse with those aspects of our psyches that we instinctively turn away from into unconsciousness is a prerequisite. And that may be plenty scary, because the feeling state that arises is the one that comes when we are willing to go down into dark, unknown, mysterious places.

The form of Buddhism that took root and flowered in Tibet from the eighth century until our day developed perhaps the most refined artistic expression of these terrifying aspects of the human psyche. Many Tibetan statues and paintings are of grotesque demonic beings, all respected members of the pantheon of honored deities. It helps to keep in mind that these deities are not gods in the usual sense. Rather, they represent different mind states, each with its own kind of divine energy that has to be faced, honored, and worked with if we are to grow and develop our true potential as full human beings. These wrathful creatures are not seen as bad, even though their appearance is frightening and repulsive, with their necklaces of skulls and grotesque grimaces. Their terrible outward appearance is actually a disguise adopted by benevolent deities embodying wisdom and compassion to help us attain greater understanding and kindness toward ourselves and others, who, it is understood, are not fundamentally different from us.

In Buddhism, the major vehicle for this work of inner development and cultivation is meditation. It is an arduous engagement, momentous one might say, all puns intended. It involves a certain degree of discipline extended over time, speaking dualistically for a moment. Similarly, in the fairy tales, as Bly pointed out, getting in touch with the wild man under the pond also requires repetitive inner work over a long time—namely, the slow bucketing out of the pond. There are no shortcuts, and nothing glamorous about bucketing out a pond by hand, or working at a hot forge or in the sweltering vineyards, day after day, year after year. But repetitive inner work of this kind, and thus engaging with and coming to know intimately the forces within one's own psyche, is its own initiation. It is a tempering process. Usually heat is involved. It takes discipline to tolerate the heat, to persevere. But what comes of keeping at it is mastery and non-naiveté, attainment of an inward order unattainable without the discipline, the heat, the descent into darkness and fear. Even the interior defeats we suffer serve us in this tempering process that sometimes really can feel like an atomic rearrangement of the crystal lattice structure of our very being and, most likely, of our body as well. Painful as it can be, it has the potential to catalyze a recognition and perhaps even an ongoing, if at first tentative, embodiment of the full dimensionality of who and what we actually already are—all coming about through knowing something firsthand of the tortuous labyrinthine depths of our own mind, as well as its boundless sky-like, space-like expanses.

The beauty of meditative adventuring is that it is possible to rely on the practice itself to guide us through the maze. It keeps us on the path, even in the darkest of moments, facing the most terrifying of our own mind states and external circumstances. It reminds us of our options. It is a guide to human development, a roadmap to our radiant selves, not to the gold of a childhood innocence already past but to that of a fully developed adult human being. But for meditation to do its work, we have to be willing to do ours. We must be willing to encounter darkness and despair when they come up and face them, over and over again if need be, without running away or numbing ourselves in the thousands of ways we habitually conjure up to avoid what is really unavoidable. Whatever arises is the curriculum of this moment. The challenge is always the same—can we meet it fully, mindfully, and heartfully?

TRY: Being open to the prince and the princess, the king and the queen, the giant and the witch, the wild man and the wild woman, the dwarf and the crone, and the warrior, the healer, and the trickster within yourself. When you meditate, put the welcome mat out for any and all of them and see what arises. Try sitting like a king or queen, a warrior or a sage. In times of great turmoil or darkness, use your breath as the string that will guide you through the labyrinth. Keep mindfulness alive even in the darkest moments, reminding yourself that awareness is not part of the darkness or the pain; it is the space that holds the pain and knows it both conceptually and nonconceptually. So awareness has to be more fundamental and closer to what is healthy and strong, golden and luminous within you.

Practice as a Path

In the middle of this road we call our life
I found myself in a dark wood
With no clear path through.

DANTE ALIGHIERI, *The Divine Comedy, Inferno*

The journey metaphor is used in all cultures to describe life and the quest for meaning. In the East, the word Tao, Chinese for "Way" or "Path," carries this meaning. In Buddhism, meditation practice is usually spoken of as a path—the path of mindfulness, the path of right understanding, the path of the wheel of truth (Dharma). More broadly, Tao and Dharma also mean the way things are, the lawfulness that governs all of existence and nonexistence. All events, whether we see them on the surface as good or bad, are fundamentally in harmony with the Tao. It is our job to learn to perceive this underlying harmony and to live and make decisions in accord with it. Yet, frequently, it is not exactly clear what the right way is, which leaves plenty of room for agency and principled action, and also for tension and controversy, to say nothing of getting lost entirely.

When we practice meditation, we are really acknowledging and reaffirming that, in this very moment, we are on the road of life. The path unfolds in walking it...with this step, in this moment, in every moment while we are alive. Meditation is more rightly thought of as a "Way" than as a technique. It is a Way of being, a

Way of living, a Way of listening, a Way of walking the path of life and being in harmony, in wise relationship, with things as they are rather than as we might idealistically want them to be. This means in part acknowledging that sometimes, often at very crucial times in life, you really have no idea where you are going or even where the path lies. At the same time, you can very well know something about where you are now (even if it is knowing that you are lost, confused, enraged, in pain, or without hope). It is not uncommon to unwittingly become trapped in a deluded belief that we do know where we are going when we really don't, especially if we are driven by self-serving ambition and we want certain things very badly, or to escape certain things very badly. There is a blindness that comes from self-furthering agendas that leaves us thinking we know when actually we don't know as much as we think.

"The Water of Life," a fairy tale in the Grimm brothers' collection from Northern Germany, tells of the customary trio of brothers, princes all. The two oldest brothers are greedy and selfish. The youngest is kind and caring. Their father, the King, is dying. An old man who mysteriously appears in the palace garden inquires after their grief and, when he hears the problem, suggests that a cure might be had in the water of life. "If the King drinks of it, he will become well again—but it is hard to find."

First, the oldest brother obtains permission to go forth to seek the water of life for his father, harboring the secret hope of currying his favor and becoming King himself. Almost as soon as he sets out on his horse, he encounters a dwarf beside the road who stops him and asks where he is going so fast. In his hurry, the brother treats the dwarf with scorn and condescension, ordering him out of his way. The presumption here is that the prince knows the way just because he knows what he is looking for. Not so. This brother is unable to rein in his arrogance, and his ignorance of the many possible ways things might unfold or open up in life at any given moment.

Of course, the dwarf in fairy tales is no outer person either but symbolic of the higher powers of the human heart, including intuition. In this case, the selfish brother is unable to approach his own inner power and feeling self with kindness and wisdom. Because of his arrogance, the dwarf arranges for his path to enter an ever-narrowing ravine, in which he eventually finds himself unable to go forward, unable to go back, and unable to turn around; in a word, stuck. And there he stays while the story continues.

When the first brother does not return, the second brother goes forth to try his luck, meets the dwarf, treats him in the same fashion, and winds up stuck just like the first brother. Because they are different parts of the same person, you might say some people never learn.

After some time, the third brother eventually sets off to bring back the water of life. He too encounters the dwarf, who asks where he is going in such a hurry. However, unlike his brothers, he stops, dismounts, and tells the dwarf of his father's grave illness and of seeking the water of life, admitting that he has no idea where to look or in what direction to go. At that, of course, the dwarf says, "Oh, I know where that is to be found," and he proceeds to tell him where it is and how he is to go about getting it, which is quite complicated. This brother listens carefully and remembers what he is told.

This richly crafted tale takes many turns in its unfolding, which I will leave to the interested reader to explore. The point here is simply that it is useful at times to admit to yourself that you don't know your way and to be open to help from unexpected places. Doing this makes available to you inner and outer energies and allies that arise out of your own heartfulness and selflessness. Of course, the selfish brothers are also aspects of the psyche. The message is that getting caught up in the normal human tendencies of self-cherishing and arrogance, and ignoring the larger order of things, will ultimately lead to an impasse in your life in which you are unable to go forward, unable to go back, and unable to turn around. The story says you will never find the water of life with such an attitude and that you will remain stuck, potentially forever.

The work of mindfulness invites recognizing, honoring, and heeding our own dwarf energy—you might say our deepest heart instincts and wisdom—rather than rushing headlong into things with a mind that is sorely out of touch with large parts of its true nature, a mind limited and driven by narrow ambition and ideas of personal gain. The story says we can only fare well if we proceed with an awareness of the way things are, including a willingness to admit not knowing where we are going. The youngest brother has a long road to travel in the story before it can be said that he fully understands the way things are (with his brothers, for instance). He endures painful lessons in treachery and betrayal, and he pays a high price for his naiveté before finally owning the full dimensionality

of his authenticity and wisdom. These are symbolized by his ultimately riding straight down the middle of a road paved in gold and
marrying the princess (I haven't told you about her) and becoming
King—not of his father's kingdom but of his own.

TRY: Seeing your own life this very day as a journey and an
adventure. Where are you heading? What are you seeking? Where
are you now? What stage of the journey have you come to? If your
life were a book, what would you call it today? What title would
you give to the chapter you are in right now? Are you stuck here in
certain ways? Can you be fully open to all of the energies at your
disposal at this point? Note that this journey is uniquely yours, no
one else's. So whatever path you choose has to be authentically
your own. You cannot imitate somebody else's trajectory and still
be true to yourself. Are you prepared to honor your uniqueness in
this way and let yourself be authentically who you already are, as
you are, in your fullness? Can you see a commitment to the meditation practice as an intimate part of this Way of being? Can you commit to lighting your way, moment by moment, with mindfulness,
with awareness? Can you see mind habits in which you could easily
get stuck, or have in the past?

Meditation: Not to Be Confused with Positive Thinking

Our ability to think the way we do differentiates our species from all others and is miraculous beyond compare. But if we are not careful, our thinking can easily crowd out other equally precious and miraculous facets of our being. Wakefulness is often the first casualty. If thinking is a superpower, which it surely is at its best, then human awareness is a superpower of even greater magnitude. Awareness eclipses thinking in its value and reach, and can transform it in the service of wisdom and compassion.

They are different forms of intelligence. Awareness is not the same as thought. It lies beyond thinking, although it can readily make use of thinking and certainly honors its value and its power. Awareness is more like a boundless container that can hold our thinking, thereby helping us to see and know our thoughts as thoughts rather than getting caught up in them as reality. Neuroscience is far from understanding awareness and how we come by it. Yet it is the signature characteristic of being human, as well as in mysterious relationship to other forms of sentience found on planet Earth.

We know that the thinking mind can at times be severely fragmented. In fact, it almost always is. This is the nature of thought. There is "this" on the one hand, and "that" on the other hand, and often a mysterious and potentially creative tension between them. But awareness, teased out of each moment with conscious intent, can help us to perceive that even in the midst of this fragmentation, our fundamental nature is already integrated and whole, and always has been. Not only is it not limited by the potpourri of our thinking mind; awareness is the pot that cradles all the fragments, just as the soup pot holds all the chopped-up carrots, peas, onions, and the like and allows them to cook into one whole, the soup itself. But it is a magical pot, much like a sorcerer's pot, because it cooks things without having to do anything, even put a fire underneath it. Awareness itself does the cooking, as long as it is sustained. You just let the fragments stir while you hold them in awareness. Whatever comes up in mind or body goes into the pot, becomes part of the soup.

Meditation does not involve trying to change your thinking by thinking some more. It involves watching thought itself. The watching is the holding. By watching your thoughts without being drawn into them (or seeing how often you are drawn into them), you can learn something profoundly liberating about thinking itself, which may help you to be less of a prisoner of those thought patterns—often so strong in us—which are narrow, inaccurate, self-involved and often self-critical, habitual to the point of being imprisoning, and almost always just plain wrong or incomplete.

One potentially helpful way to understand meditation is to view the process of thinking itself as a waterfall, a continual cascading of thoughts, one right after another. In cultivating mindfulness, we are settling in behind our thinking, much the way you might find a vantage point in a cave or depression in the rock behind a waterfall. We still see and hear the water, but we are safely out of the torrent.

Practicing in this way, our thought patterns change by themselves in ways that nourish integration, understanding, and compassion in our lives, but not because we are trying to make them change by replacing one thought with another one that we think may be better or somehow more pure. Rather, it is to understand the nature of our thoughts as thoughts—as discrete and impersonal events arising in the field of awareness—and our relationship to them, so that they can be more at our service rather than the other way round.

If we decide to think positively, that may be useful, but it is not meditation. It is just more thinking. We can as easily become a prisoner of so-called positive thinking as we can of negative thinking. It too can be confining, fragmented, inaccurate, illusory, self-serving, and wrong. Another element altogether is required to induce transformation in our lives and take us beyond the limits of thought.

Going Inside

It is easy to come by the impression that meditation is about going inside or dwelling inside yourself. But "inside" and "outside" are limited distinctions. In the stillness of formal practice, we do turn our energies inward, only to discover that we contain the entire universe in our own mind and body.

Dwelling inwardly for extended periods, we come to know something of the poverty of always looking outside ourselves for happiness, understanding, and wisdom. It's not that God, the environment, and other people cannot help us to be happy or to find satisfaction. It's just that our happiness, satisfaction, and our understanding will be no deeper than our capacity to know ourselves inwardly, to encounter the outer world from the deep comfort that comes from being at home in one's own skin, from an intimate familiarity with the ways of one's own mind and body.

Inviting the body to settle into stillness and simply taking up residence in awareness for some part of each day, we touch what is most real and reliable in ourselves and most easily overlooked and undeveloped. When we can be at home with and in ourselves, even for brief periods of time in the face of the pull of the outer world, not having to look elsewhere for something to fill us up, or make us happy, or get us to the next moment, we can be at home wherever we find ourselves, at peace with things as they are, moment by moment.

*

Don't go outside your house to see the flowers.
My friend, don't bother with that excursion.
Inside your body there are flowers.
One flower has a thousand petals.
That will do for a place to sit.
Sitting there you will have a glimpse of beauty
inside the body and out of it,
before gardens and after gardens.

KABIR

*

The heavy is the root of the light.
The unmoved is the source of all movement.
Thus the Master travels all day
without leaving home.
However splendid the views,
she stays serenely in herself.
Why should the lord of the country
flit about like a fool?
If you let yourself be blown to and fro,
you lose touch with your root.

If you let restlessness move you,

you lose touch with who you are.

LAO-TZU, *Tao-te-Ching*

*

Direct your eye right inward, and you'll find

A thousand regions in your mind

Yet undiscovered. Travel them and be

Expert in home-cosmography.

THOREAU, *Walden*

TRY: The next time you feel a sense of dissatisfaction, of something being missing or not quite right, turn inward just as an experiment. See if you can capture the energy of that very moment. Instead of reaching for your phone or distracting yourself in some other way, make room for yourself to just be in the moment with things being exactly as they are, whether they are pleasant, unpleasant, or neutral. Sit down and enter into the stream of your breathing, if only for a few minutes. Don't look for anything—neither flowers nor light nor a beautiful view. Don't extol the virtues of anything or condemn the inadequacy of anything. Don't even think to yourself, "I am going inward now." Just sit. Reside at the center of the world, with things exactly as they are.

PART TWO

The Heart of Practice

What lies behind us and what lies before us are tiny matters compared to what lies within us.

Sitting Meditation

What is so special about sitting? Nothing, when we speak of the way we ordinarily sit. It's just one convenient way our bodies take a load off our feet. But when it comes to meditation, sitting is very special.

You can know that superficially easily enough from the outside. For instance, you might not know that a person is meditating when you see them standing or lying down or walking, but you know it immediately when the person is sitting, especially if it is on the floor. From any angle, the posture itself embodies wakefulness and presence, even when the eyes are closed and the face is serene and peaceful. It is mountainlike in its uncontrived majesty and solidity. There is a stability to it that speaks volumes. The moment the person dozes off, all those qualities evaporate. The mind collapses inwardly, the body visibly.

Sitting meditation involves establishing yourself in an upright, dignified posture and then maintaining it, often for extended periods of time. Although it is relatively easy to assume an erect posture, that is just the beginning of this challenging process of continual unfolding. You may readily enough "park" your body, but there is still the question of what the mind is up to. Sitting meditation is not a matter of taking on a special body posture, however powerful that may be. It invites you to adopt a particular posture toward the mind. It is mind sitting.

Once you are sitting, there are many ways to approach the present moment. All involve paying attention on purpose, non-judgmentally. What varies is what you attend to and how. But keep in mind that *it is the attending itself that is most important, not the object of attention*, whatever it might be.

It is best to keep things simple and start close to home, with your body and the sensations of breathing—attending to them wherever they are most vivid as the breath moves in and out. Ultimately, you can expand your awareness to observe all the comings and goings, the gyrations and machinations of your own thoughts and feelings, perceptions and impulses, body and mind and world. But it may take some time for concentration and mindfulness to become stable enough to hold such a wide range of objects in awareness, often changing rapidly, without getting lost in them, or attached to particular ones, or simply overwhelmed. For most of us, it takes years and depends in large measure on your motivation and your willingness to let things be as they are and not force anything—staying as faithful as you can to the commitment to keep up formal practice over days, weeks, months, years, and decades, no matter what. At the beginning, you might want to focus primarily on the breath sensations in the body, wherever they are most vivid, and use them as an anchor to bring you back whenever you find your attention has been carried away. Try it for a few years and see what happens.

TRY: Setting aside a time every day for just being. Five minutes would be fine, or ten or twenty or thirty if you want to venture that far. Sit down and watch the timeless moments unfold, with no agenda other than to be fully present. Use the breath sensations in the body to tether your attention to the present moment. Your thinking mind will drift here and there, depending on the currents and winds moving in the mind until, at some point, the anchor line grows taut and brings you back. This will happen a lot. Bring your attention back to the breath in the body, perhaps in the belly, in all its sensory vividness, every time it wanders off. As best as you can, intend for the posture to be erect and dignified, not rigid or stiff. It might help to think of yourself as a mountain.

Since every mountain is unique and different on all sides, let your body dictate how it will manifest your intention to be present sitting—if sitting is possible for you at all—whether it be on the floor with appropriate cushioning (usually a zafu on top of a zabuton) or on a straight-backed chair. If that is too constrained or challenging for your body's unique condition or needs, be creative. Instead of a mountain, try becoming a tree, or a boulder, or a frog on a lily pad. Whatever speaks to and supports the condition of your body is the right doorway into formal practice.

Taking Your Seat

It helps to come to the cushion or to the chair with a definite sense of taking your seat. Sitting meditation is different from just sitting down casually somewhere. There is energy in the statement the sitting makes as you take your seat, both in the choice of spot and in mindfulness filling your body. The posture embodies "taking a stand," even though you are sitting. There is a strong sense of honoring place and placement of body and mind and your motivation in that moment. Certainly, every time you take your seat, you are taking a stand in your life in favor of embodied wakefulness, not in some future moment, but right now. So it helps to adopt a sitting posture that embodies that intentionality. Let it be a radical act—of sanity, of love. As best you can, let it be simultaneously firm and gentle, without any forcing or contrivance.

We take our seat to meditate keeping all this in mind but without any undue investment in location or posture. There may indeed be definite "power spots" indoors and out, yet with this attitude of taking a stand, you can sit anywhere in any posture and be at home. When your mind and body collaborate in holding body, time, place, and posture in awareness, and remain unattached to it having to be a certain way, then and only then are you truly sitting.

Dignity

When describing the sitting posture, the word that feels the most appropriate to me is "dignity."

Sitting down to meditate, the posture we assume speaks to us. It makes its own statement. You might say the posture itself is the meditation. If we slump, it reflects low energy, passivity, a lack of clarity. If we sit ramrod-straight, we are tense, making too much of an effort, trying too hard. When I use the word "dignity" in teaching situations, as in "Let's sit in a way that embodies dignity," everybody immediately adjusts their posture to sit up straighter. But they don't stiffen. Faces relax; shoulders drop; head, neck, and back come into easy alignment. The spine rises out of the pelvis with energy. Sometimes people tend to sit forward, away from the backs of their chairs, more autonomously. Everybody seems to instantly know that inner feeling of dignity and how to embrace and embody it.

Perhaps we just need little reminders from time to time that we are already dignified, already deserving, already worthy. Sometimes we don't feel that way because of the wounds and the scars we carry from the past or because of the uncertainty of the future. It is doubtful that we came to feel undeserving on our own. We were helped to feel unworthy. We were taught it in a thousand ways when we were little, and we learned our lessons well.

So, when we take our seat in meditation and remind ourselves to sit in a posture that embodies wakefulness and dignity, we are coming back to our original worthiness, to our original beauty. That in itself is quite a statement. You can bet our inside will be listening. Are we ready to listen, too? Are we ready to listen to the currents of direct experience in this moment, and this one, and this one...?

TRY: Sitting with dignity for a full minute. Note how you feel. Try standing with dignity. Where are your shoulders? How is your pelvis, your spine, your head? How are your legs and your feet? What would it mean to walk with dignity?

Posture

When you sit with strong intentionality, the body itself makes a statement of deep conviction and commitment in its carriage. These qualities of heart and mind radiate inward and outward. A dignified sitting posture is itself an affirmation of freedom and of life's harmony, beauty, and richness right here and right now.

Sometimes you feel in touch with it; other times you may not. Even when you feel depressed, burdened, confused, sitting can affirm the strength and value of this life lived now. If you can muster the patience to sustain your sitting for even a brief time, it can bring you in touch with the essential nature of your being, beyond feeling up or down, free or burdened, clear-sighted or confused. This elemental nature is akin to awareness itself; it doesn't fluctuate with mental state or life circumstances. It is mirrorlike, impartially reflecting what comes before it. This includes a deep knowing that whatever is present, whatever has happened to shake your life or overwhelm you, will of itself inevitably change and, for this reason alone, bears simply holding in the mirror of the present moment. This might take the form of watching it, embracing its presence, riding its waves of unfolding just as you ride the waves of your own breathing, knowing that, sooner or later, you will find a way to act, to come to terms with, to move into, and through, and beyond whatever you are carrying. Not by trying so much as by attending, by letting things be and feeling them fully moment by moment.

111

Mindful sitting meditation is not an attempt to escape from problems or difficulties into some cut-off "meditative" state of absorption or denial. On the contrary, it is a willingness to go nose to nose with pain, confusion, and loss, if that is what is dominating the present moment, and to stay with the observing over a sustained period of time, underneath whatever thoughts and emotions are moving through the mind. If any understanding is to arise, it will come in its own time simply through bearing the situation in mind, along with your breath, as you maintain the sitting posture.

In the Zen tradition, one teacher (Shunryu Suzuki Roshi) put it this way: "The state of mind that exists when you sit in the right posture is itself enlightenment.... These forms [sitting meditation] are not the means of obtaining the right state of mind. To take this posture is itself the right state of mind." In the sitting meditation, you are already touching your own truest nature.

So, when we practice sitting meditation, first and foremost it means sitting in such a way that your body affirms, radiates, broadcasts an attitude of presence, that you are committed to acknowledging and accepting whatever comes up in any moment. This orientation is one of nonattachment and unwavering stability, like a clear mirror, only reflecting, itself empty, receptive, open. This attitude is intrinsic to the posture and in the very way you take your seat. The posture itself embodies the attitude—especially if it is unforced, uncontrived.

That is why many people find the image of a mountain helpful in deepening concentration and mindfulness in the sitting practice. Invoking qualities of elevation, massiveness, majesty, unmovingness, rootedness, and stability helps bring these qualities directly into one's posture and attitude.

It is important to invite these qualities into your meditation all the time. Practicing over and over again embodying dignity, stillness, an unwavering equanimity in the face of any mind state that presents itself, especially when you are not in a grave state of distress or turmoil, can provide a solid, reliable foundation for maintaining mindfulness and equanimity, even in periods of extreme stress and emotional turmoil. But only if you practice, practice, practice.

Although it is tempting to do so, you can't just think that you understand how to be mindful and save using it for only those moments when the big events hit. They contain so much power they will overwhelm you instantly, along with all your romantic ideas about equanimity and knowing how to be mindful. Meditation practice is the slow, disciplined work of digging trenches, of working in the vineyards, of bucketing out a pond, of getting your rear end on the cushion, so to speak, literally and metaphorically, and keeping it there, perhaps for longer than feels comfortable at times. It is the work of no time and the work of a lifetime, all wrapped into one seamless whole.

What to Do with Your Hands

Various subtle energy pathways in the body have been mapped out, understood, and used in particular ways in the yogic and meditative traditions for millennia. We intuitively know that all our body postures make their own unique statements, which radiate inwardly as well as outwardly. The outward aspect goes by the term "body language." We can use that language to read how other people feel about themselves, because people are continuously broadcasting such information for anyone with a sensitive enough receiver to pick it up.

But in this case, we are speaking of the value of becoming sensitive to the language of one's own body, in other words, the inward aspect. Here, awareness can catalyze dramatic inner growth and transformation. In the yogic traditions, this domain of mindfulness and intentionality includes certain configurations of the body known as mudras. In a way, all postures are mudras: each makes a particular statement and has a characteristic energy associated with it. But mudras are usually referencing something more subtle than the posture of the entire body. Their focus is primarily on the positioning of the hands and feet.

If you go to a museum and carefully observe the Buddhist paintings and statues, you will quickly notice that in the hundreds of different depictions of meditation, whether sitting, standing, or lying down, the hands are in a range of different positions. In the case of sitting meditation, sometimes the hands are on the knees, palms down; sometimes one or both palms are up; sometimes one or more fingers of one hand are touching the ground, while the other hand is raised up. Sometimes the hands are together in the lap, with the fingers of one hand lying atop the fingers of the other, the thumb tips gently touching as if circling an invisible egg to form what is called the "cosmic mudra." Sometimes the fingers and palms are placed together over the heart, as in the traditional posture of Christian prayer. This same posture, in Asian cultures, is a form of greeting, a mutual bow of recognition of the divinity within the other person and of the sanctity of the relationship.

These hand mudras all carry different energies that you can experiment with in your meditation practice. Try sitting with your hands palms down on your knees. Notice the quality of self-containment here. To me, this posture speaks of not looking for anything more but simply being complete with what is.

If you then mindfully turn both palms up, you may note a change in energy in the body. To me, sitting this way embodies receptivity, an openness to what is above, to the spaciousness of the heavens. Sometimes I feel a strong impulse to open to energy from above. It can be quite helpful at times, especially in periods of turmoil or confusion, to intentionally embody receptivity in your sitting practice. This can be done simply by opening your palms to the heavens. It's not that you are actively looking for something to magically help you. Rather, you are making yourself available to higher-dimensional insights, priming a willingness in yourself to resonate with energies we usually think of as elevated, divine, celestial, cosmic, universal, of a higher order and wisdom.

All hand postures can be thought of as mudras, in that they are associated with subtle or not-so-subtle energies. Take the energy of the fist, for instance. When we get angry, our jaw tends to clench and our hands tend to close into fists. Some people unknowingly practice this mudra a lot in their lives. Of course, that gesture only waters whatever incipient seeds of anger and violence are within you every time you engage in it, and those seeds, unfortunately, respond by sprouting and growing stronger.

The next time you find yourself making fists out of anger, try to bring mindfulness to the inner attitude embodied in a fist. Feel the tension, the rage, the hatred, the anger, the aggression, and the fear it contains. Then, in the midst of your anger, as an experiment, if the person you are angry at is present, try opening your fists and placing the palms together over your heart in the prayer position right in front of them. (Of course, they won't have the slightest idea what you are doing.) Notice what happens to the anger and hurt as you hold this position for even a few moments.

I find it virtually impossible to sustain anger when I do this. It's not that the anger may not be justified. It's just that all sorts of other feelings come into play, which frame the anger energy and tame it—feelings like empathy and compassion for the other person, and perhaps a greater understanding of the dance we are both caught up in.... The dance of one thing inevitably leading to another, of the concatenation of consequences impersonally set in motion, the end result of which can (mistakenly) be taken personally and lead to ignorance compounding ignorance, aggression compounding aggression, with no wisdom or kindness anywhere.

When Gandhi was assassinated at point-blank range, he put his palms together in this way toward his attacker, uttered his mantra, and died. Years of meditation and yoga practice, guided by his beloved Bhagavad Gita, had brought him to the point where he was able to bring the perspective of nonattachment to everything he was engaged in, including his very life. It allowed him to choose the attitude he would take in that very moment he was being robbed of life. He didn't die angry or even surprised. He had known his life was in constant danger. But he had trained himself to march to the drumbeat of his own growing vision of what constituted wise action. Although he had his own areas of idiosyncratic stubbornness, he had come to a point where he embodied compassion, along with an unwavering commitment to both political and spiritual freedom. His personal wellbeing was of limited value in comparison. He was always putting it on the line.

TRY: Being aware of subtle emotional qualities you may be embodying or even broadcasting, at various times of the day, as well as during your formal sitting practice. Pay particular attention to your hands. Does their position make a difference? See if you don't become more mindful by becoming more "bodyful" in such moments.

As you practice being more in touch with your hands during periods of sitting meditation, see whether this doesn't have an influence on the way you touch. Everything from opening a door to making love involves touch. It is possible to open a door so mindlessly that your hand doesn't know what the rest of your body is doing and you wind up actually walking into it, or hitting your head. Imagine the challenge of touching another person without automaticity, with no gaining idea, just fully present, and caring.

Coming Out of Meditation

The moments toward the end of a period of formal meditation have their own tricky topology. Mindfulness can become lax with the anticipation of finishing. How you handle this is important. It is precisely such transitions that challenge us to deepen our practice and extend its range.

Toward the end of a period of formal practice, if you are not particularly attentive, before you know it you'll be off doing something else, with no awareness whatsoever of how the meditation came to an end. The transition will be a blur at best. You can bring mindfulness to this process by being in touch with the thoughts and impulses that tell you it's time to stop. Whether you've been still for an hour or for three minutes, a powerful feeling all of a sudden may say, "This is enough." Or you look at your watch and it's the time you said you would quit.

In your meditation practice, especially when you are not using audio guidance of some kind, see if you can detect the very first impulse to quit and any others that may follow, growing in strength. As you recognize each impulse, breathe with it for a few moments, and ask yourself, "Who has had enough?" Try looking into what is behind the impulse. Is it fatigue, boredom, pain, impatience, or is it just time to stop? Whatever the case, rather than automatically leaping up or moving on, try lingering with whatever arises out of this inquiry, breathing with it for a few moments or even longer and allowing the moving out of your meditation posture to be as much an object of moment-to-moment awareness as any other moment in the meditation.

Practicing like this can refine the quality of sensitivity and awareness we bring to many different situations that involve closing or ending something and moving on to something else. It can be as simple and brief as being in touch with closing a door or as complicated and painful as when an era in your life comes to an end. So much automaticity can creep into closing a door, because it's so unimportant in the overall scheme of things (unless the baby is sleeping or someone is sick in the house). But it is precisely because it is relatively unimportant that closing the door mindfully activates and deepens our sensitivity, our capacity to be in touch with all of our moments, and smooths out some of the deeper wrinkles of our habitual unconsciousness.

Curiously, just as much if not more mindless behavior can creep into our most momentous closures and life transitions, including our own aging and our own dying. Here, too, mindfulness can have healing effects. We may be so defended against feeling the full impact of our emotional pain—whether it be fear, grief, sadness, shame, disappointment, anger, or for that matter, even joy or satisfaction—that we unconsciously escape into a cloud of numbness in which we do not permit ourselves to feel anything at all or know what we are feeling. Like a fog, unawareness blankets precisely those moments that might be the most profound occasions to see impermanence at work; to be in touch with the universal and impersonal aspects of being and becoming that underlie our personalized emotional investments; to touch the mystery of being small, fragile, and temporary; and to come to peace with the absolute inevitability of change and endings.

In the Zen tradition, group sitting meditations are sometimes ended with a loud wooden clacker that is whacked together forcefully. No romantic lingering with the sound of a soft bell to ease the end of a sitting. The message here is to cut—time to move on now. If you're daydreaming, even slightly, when the clacker goes off, the sound will startle you and thereby point out how little you were actually present in that moment. It reminds you that the sitting is already over and now we are in a new moment, to be faced anew.

In other traditions, the gentle ring of a bell or gong is used to mark the end of group sittings. It is the softness of the sound that brings you back, and also reveals whether your mind was on the loose at the moment it rang. So, when it comes to ending a sitting, soft and gentle is good, and hard and loud is good. Both remind us to be fully present in moments of transition, that all endings are also beginnings, that what is most important—in the phrase from the Diamond Sutra that so affected Hui-neng centuries ago and set him on his path—is to "develop a mind that clings to nothing." Only then will we be able to see things as they actually are and respond with the full range of our emotional capacity and our wisdom.

*

The Master sees things as they are,
without trying to control them.
She lets them go their own way,
and resides at the center of the circle.

LAO-TZU, *Tao-te-Ching*

TRY: Bringing awareness to how you end your meditations. Whether you are lying down, sitting, standing, or walking, zero in on "who" ends it, how it ends, when it ends, and why. Don't judge it or yourself in any way—just observe and stay in touch with the transition from one thing to the next, reminding yourself that the real meditation practice is life itself, not merely your times of formal practice. So a seamless continuity of awareness across transitions, endings and beginnings, might be interesting to explore.

How Long to Practice?

Q: "Dr. Kabat-Zinn, how long should I meditate?"
A: "How should I know?"

It keeps coming up, this question of how long to meditate. I felt strongly right from the beginning of the work of MBSR that it would be important for the people with medical conditions referred to the program by their doctors and other health-care providers to be exposed from the start to relatively extended periods of formal practice. In fact, taking the MBSR program requires an immediate lifestyle change in the form of devoting forty-five minutes per day, six days per week, to various formal meditation practices over the eight weeks of the program. And we very explicitly state that "you don't have to like it; you just have to do it for the eight weeks of the program. At the end, you can tell us whether it was valuable or not—but not in between." That was the deal, and people were happy to give it a go under those conditions. It was an investment, so to speak, in themselves and what might be possible. And MBSR is still that way, almost forty-five years later.

The basic principle from the get-go was this: If you ask a lot of people or they are motivated to ask a lot of themselves, especially over a relatively short period of eight weeks, then you may get a lot. But if you ask a little, the most you are likely to get is the little that you asked for.

Forty-five minutes seemed long enough to settle into stillness and sustained attending from moment to moment, and perhaps to experience at least tastes of a settling or quieting of the mind, a deepening comfort in residing in the present moment with no agenda, and a sense of momentary wellbeing. It also seemed long enough to allow for ample opportunity to engage with the more challenging mind states that we ordinarily hope to avoid because they take over our lives and severely tax (when they don't overwhelm completely) our ability to remain calm, mindful, and accepting. The usual suspects, of course, when it comes to challenging mind states are boredom, impatience, frustration, fear, anxiety (which would include worrying about all the things you might be accomplishing if you weren't wasting time meditating), fantasy, memories, anger, pain, fatigue, and grief.

It turned out to be a good intuition. Most of the people coming through the MBSR program willingly make the almost never easy adjustments in the day-to-day conduct of their lives to practice daily for forty-five minutes at a stretch, at least over a period of eight weeks. And many never stray from that new life path. It not only becomes easy; it becomes necessary, a lifeline, and a new way of being in your life, of inhabiting your day.

But there is a flip side to this way of looking at things. What may be challenging but doable for one person at one time in their life may be nigh impossible at another time even for that same person. Perceptions of "long" and "short" are at best relative. The single mother of small children is unlikely to have forty-five minutes at a stretch for anything. Does that mean she can't meditate?

If your life is in perpetual crisis or you find yourself immersed in social and economic chaos, you may have trouble finding the psychic energy to meditate formally for extended periods, even if you have the time. Something always seems to come up to get in the way, especially if you are thinking you have to have a forty-five-minute clearing in your day even to get started. Practicing in cramped quarters around the lives of other family members can make for uncomfortable feelings that can easily become significant obstacles to daily practice.

Medical students can hardly be expected routinely to carve out extended periods for non-doing, nor can many other people in high-stress jobs and demanding situations. Nor can folks who are just curious about meditation but have no strong reason to push the limits of convenience and of their own sense of time pressure or comfort.

For those seeking balance in their lives, a certain flexibility of approach is not only helpful; it is essential. It is important to know that meditation has little to do with clock time. Five minutes of formal practice can be as profound as forty-five minutes, maybe even more so. The sincerity of your effort matters far more than elapsed time, since we are really talking about stepping out of minutes and hours and into moments, which are truly dimensionless and therefore infinite. So, if you have some motivation to practice even a little, that is what is important. Mindfulness needs to be kindled and nurtured, protected from the winds of a busy life or a restless and tormented mind, just as a small flame needs to be sheltered from strong gusts of air.

If you can manage only five minutes, or even one minute, of mindfulness at first, that is truly wonderful. It means you have already remembered the value of stopping, of shifting even momentarily from doing to being.

When we teach meditation to medical students to help them with the stress and sometimes the trauma of medical education in its present form, or to college athletes who want to train their minds along with their bodies to optimize performance, or to people in a pulmonary rehabilitation program who need to learn how to befriend and work with their breathing in new ways through meditation, or to employees in a lunchtime stress reduction class, we don't insist on forty-five minutes of practice a day. (We do that only with our own patients or with people who are ready to make such an intense lifestyle change for reasons of their own.) Instead, we challenge them to practice every day for fifteen minutes at a time, or twice a day if they can manage that.

If you think about it for a moment, few of us—no matter what we do or what situation we find ourselves in—would be unable to free up one or two fifteen-minute blocks of time out of twenty-four hours. And if not fifteen, then ten, or five.

Recall that in a line six inches long, there are an infinite number of points, and in a line one inch long there are just as many. Well, then, how many moments are there in fifteen minutes, or five, or ten, or forty-five? It turns out we have plenty of time, if we are willing to hold any moments at all in awareness.

Forming the intention to practice and then seizing a moment—any moment—and embracing it fully in your inward and outward posture lies at the core of the cultivation of mindfulness in terms of formal meditation practice. Long and short periods of practice are both good, but "long" may never flourish if your frustration and the obstacles in your path loom too large. Far better to venture into longer periods of practice gradually on your own or on a retreat than never to taste mindfulness or stillness because the perceived obstacles were too great. A journey of a thousand miles really does begin with a single step. When we commit to taking that step—in this case, to taking our seat for even the briefest of times—we can touch the timeless in any moment. From that all benefit flows, and from that alone.

*

When you really look for me, you will see me instantly—you will find me in the tiniest house of time.

KABIR

TRY: Sitting for varying lengths of clock time. See how it affects your practice. Does your concentration lapse as you sit longer? Do you get caught up in how much longer you "have" to go before the bell rings or your time is up? Does impatience arise at some point? Does the mind get reactive or obsessive? Is there restlessness? Anxiety? Boredom? Time pressure? Sleepiness? Dullness? If you are new to meditation, are you finding yourself saying, "This is stupid" or "Am I doing it right?" or "Is this all I am supposed to be experiencing?"

Do these feelings start right away, or do they come up only after a while? Are you able to see them merely as transient and totally impersonal mind states, even if their content and emotional charge is overwhelmingly about "you"? Can you observe them without judging them or yourself for even brief periods? If you put the welcome mat out for them (a very good thing to try in general) and investigate their content, qualities, and emotional charge—and let them be—you may learn a lot about what is strong and unwavering in yourself. And what is strong in you will invariably become even stronger as you intentionally nourish inner stability and calm.

No One Right Way

Backpacking with my family in Teton Wilderness, I am recurrently struck by the question of footing. With each step, the foot has to come down somewhere. Climbing or descending over boulder fields, steep inclines, on and off trails, our feet make split-second decisions for us about where and how to come down, what angle, how much pressure, heel or toe, rotated or straight. The kids don't ever ask, "Daddy, where do I put my feet? Should I step on this rock or that one?" They just do it, and I've noticed that they find a way—they choose where to put their feet at each step, and it's not simply where I put mine.

What this says to me is that our feet find their own way. Watching my own, I am amazed at how many different places and ways I might put my foot down with each step, and how out of this unfolding momentary potential, the foot ultimately commits to one way, executes with full weight on it (or less if it's a hazardous situation), and then lets go as the other foot makes its choice and I move forward. All this occurs virtually without thinking, except at the occasional tricky spots where thought and experience do come into play and I might have to give my youngest a hand. But that is the exception, not the rule. Ordinarily we are not looking at our feet and thinking about each step. We are looking out, ahead on the trail, and our brain, taking it all in, makes split-second decisions for us that put the foot down in a way that conforms to the needs of the terrain underfoot in that moment.

This doesn't mean that there is no wrong way to step. You do have to be careful and sense your footing. It's just that the eyes and the brain are very good at rapid assessment of terrain and giving detailed directions to torso, limbs, and feet, so that the whole process of taking a step on rough ground is one of exquisite balance in motion, even with the complication of boots and heavy packs. There is built-in mindfulness here. Rough terrain brings it out in us. And if we do a trail ten times, we'll each solve the problem of each footstep differently each time. Covering ground on foot always unfolds out of the uniqueness of the present moment and out of our inborn intelligences that make it possible and mostly effortless.

It's no different in meditation. There is really and truly no one "right way" to practice, although there are plenty of wrong ways and many pitfalls along this path as well, and they have to be looked out for. It is best to encounter each moment with freshness, its rich potential held in awareness. We look deeply into it, and then we let go into the next moment, not holding on to the last one but aware of the fleeting memory trace and what might be learned from it. Each moment then can be fresh, each inbreath a new beginning, each outbreath a new letting go, a new letting be. Just as with stepping over rocky terrain, mysteriously in touch with the affordances,* there is no "supposed to" here. True, there is much to be seen and understood along this path, but it can't be forced any more than you can force someone to appreciate the golden light of the low sun

---

* See S. Grafton, *Physical Intelligence: The Science of How the Body and the Mind Guide Each Other Through Life*, Pantheon, New York, 2020.

shining over fields of wheat or the moonrise in the mountains. Best not to speak at all in such moments. All you can do is be present with the enormity of it yourself and hope others see it in the silence of the moment. Sunsets and moonrises speak for themselves, in their own languages, on their own canvases. Silence at times leaves space for the untamed and the unnamed to speak.

In the same way, in the meditation practice, it is best to honor one's own direct experience and not worry too much about whether this (whatever the *this* is) is what you are supposed to feel or see or think about. Why not trust your experience in this moment just as you would trust your foot to find a way to keep you balanced as you move over rocks? If you practice this kind of trust in the face of insecurity and the strong habit of wanting some authority to anoint your experience (however minuscule, and it usually is) with their blessing, you will find that something of a deepening and ripening nature does happen along the arc of a lifetime of practice. Our feet and our breath both teach us to watch our step, to proceed mindfully, to be truly at home in every moment, wherever our feet carry us, to appreciate where we are. What greater gift could be bestowed upon us?

TRY: Being aware of all the times in meditation when the thought comes up, "Am I doing this right?" "Is this what I should be feeling?" "Is this what is 'supposed' to happen?" Instead of trying to answer these questions, just look more deeply into the present moment. Expand your awareness in this very moment. Hold the question in awareness along with your breathing and with the full range of this particular moment's context. Trust that in this moment, "This is it," whatever and wherever the "this" is. Looking deeply into whatever arises, as best you can keep up a continuity in the practice, allowing one moment to unfold into the next without analyzing, discoursing, judging, condemning, or doubting; simply observing, embracing, opening, letting be, accepting. Right now. Only this step. Only this moment.

A What-Is-My-Way? Meditation

We are quick to tell little children that they can't always have their own way, even implying that there is something wrong with wanting it. And when they ask, "Why not, Mommy?" "Why not, Daddy?" and we have come to the end of our explanations or our patience, we are likely to say, "Never mind. Just listen to me. You'll understand when you grow up."

But isn't this more than a little unfair? Don't we adults behave in exactly the same way as our children? Don't we want to have things our own way too, all the time if possible? How are we different from children except that we are less honest and open about it? And what if we could have our own way? What would it be? Do you remember the trouble that people get into in fairy tales when they are offered three wishes by a genie or a dwarf or a witch?

The people of Maine are known for saying, "You can't get there from here," when asked for directions. In terms of life directions, perhaps it is truer to say, "You can only get there if you are fully here." How many of us are aware of this little twist in the fabric of fate? Would we know what our way is if we could have it? Would getting our way solve anything at all, or would it only make more of a mess of our lives were it possible to realize our wishes on impulse out of our so frequently mindless states of mind?

The truly interesting question here is, "What exactly is my way?" meaning my Way with a capital W. Rarely do we contemplate our life with this degree of inquiry and probing. How frequently do we linger in such basic questions as "Who am I?" "Where am I going?" "What trajectory am I on?" "Is this the right direction for me?" "If I could choose a path now, in which direction would I head?" "What do I long for?" "What do I truly love?"

Contemplating "What is my Way?" is an excellent element to inject into our meditation practice. We don't have to come up with answers or think that there has to be one particular answer. Better not to think at all. Instead, only persist in asking the question, letting any answers that formulate just come of themselves and go of themselves. As with everything else in the meditation practice, we just watch, listen, note, let be, let go, and keep generating the question..."What is my Way?" "What is my path?" "Who am I?"

The intention here is to remain open to *not knowing*, perhaps allowing yourself to come to the point of admitting, "I don't know," and then experimenting with relaxing a bit into this not-knowing instead of condemning yourself for it. After all, in this moment, it may be an accurate statement of how things are for you.

Inquiry and investigations of this kind can give rise to openings, to new understandings and visions and actions. Inquiry takes on a life of its own after a while. It permeates the pores of your being and breathes new vitality, vibrancy, and grace into the bland, the humdrum, the routine. Inquiry will wind up "doing you" rather than you doing it. This is a good way to find and walk the path that lies closest to your heart. After all, the journey is one of heroic proportions—but so much more so if enlivened by wakefulness and a commitment to adventurous inquiry and continual openness to what is called for now. As a human being, you are the central figure in the universal hero's mythic journey, the fairy tale, the Arthurian quest. For all of us, this journey is the trajectory between birth and death, a human life lived. No one escapes the adventure. We only work with it differently.

Can we be in touch with our own life unfolding? Can we rise to the all-too-fleeting occasion of our own humanity, recognizing our intrinsic goodness, our strengths, and our beauty? Can we take on the challenges we meet, even seeking them out to test ourselves, to grow, to act in a principled way, to be true to ourselves, to find our own Way and ultimately not only have it but, more importantly, live it?

The Mountain Meditation

When it comes to meditation, mountains have a lot to teach, having archetypal significance in all cultures. Mountains are sacred places. People have always sought guidance and renewal in and among them. The mountain is the prime axis of the world (Mt. Meru); the dwelling place of the gods (Mt. Olympus); the place the spiritual leader encounters God, receives commandments, and forges a covenant (Mt. Sinai); the oldest child of Wakea and Papawalinu'u, the male and female sources of all life (Mauna Kea). Mountains are held sacred, embodying dread and harmony, harshness and majesty, sources of clouds and rainfall, of life itself. Rising above all else on our planet, they beckon, overwhelm, and inspire awe in their sheer presence. Their nature is elemental, rock. Rock hard. Rock solid. Mountains are the place of visions, where one can touch the panoramic scale of the natural world and its intersection with life's fragile but tenacious rootings. Mountains have played key roles in history and prehistory. To traditional peoples, mountains were and still are mother, father, guardian, protector, ally.

In meditation practice, it can be helpful sometimes to respectfully "borrow" these wonderful archetypal qualities of mountains and use them to bolster our intentionality and resolve to hold the moment with an elemental purity and simplicity, even sacredness. The mountain image held in the mind's eye and in the body can freshen our memory of why we are sitting in the first place, and of what it truly means, each time we take our seat, to dwell in the realm of non-doing. Mountains are quintessentially emblematic of abiding presence and stillness, of both constancy and change.

The mountain meditation can be practiced in the following way, or modified to resonate with your personal vision of the mountain, any mountain, and its meaning to you. It can be invoked in any posture. But, that said, I find it most powerful when I am sitting cross-legged on the floor so that my body looks and feels most mountainlike, inwardly and outwardly. Being in the mountains or in sight of a mountain is helpful but not at all necessary. It is the inner image that is your ally and the source of empowerment here.

Picture the most beautiful mountain you know or know of or can imagine, one whose form speaks personally to you. As you focus on the image or the feeling of the mountain in your mind's eye, notice its overall shape, the lofty peak, the base rooted in the rock of the earth's crust, the steep or gently sloping sides. Note as well how massive it is, how unmoving, how beautiful whether seen from afar or up close—a beauty emanating from its unique signature of shape and form, and at the same time embodying universal qualities of "mountainness" transcending particular shape and form.

Perhaps your mountain has snow at the top and trees on the lower slopes. Perhaps it has one prominent peak, perhaps a series of peaks or a high plateau. However it appears, just sit and breathe with the image of this mountain, observing it, noting its contours, its various qualities.

When you feel ready, see if you can bring the mountain into your own body so that your body sitting here and the mountain of the mind's eye become one. Your head becomes the lofty peak, your shoulders and arms the sides of the mountain, your buttocks and legs the solid base rooted to your cushion on the floor or to your chair. Experience in your body the sense of uplift, the axial, elevated quality of the mountain deep in your own pelvis and spine. Invite yourself to become a breathing mountain, unwavering in your stillness, completely what you are—beyond words and thought, a centered, rooted, unmoving presence.

Now, as well you know, throughout the day, as the sun travels the sky, the mountain just sits. Light and shadow and colors are changing virtually moment to moment in the mountain's adamantine stillness. Even the untrained eye can see changes by the hour. These evoke those masterpieces of Claude Monet, who had the genius to set up many easels and paint the life of his inanimate subjects hour by hour, moving from canvas to canvas as the play of light, shadow, and color transformed cathedral, river, or mountain, and thereby woke up the viewer's eye. As the light changes, as night follows day and day night, the mountain just sits, simply being itself. It remains still as the seasons flow into one another and as the weather changes moment by moment and day by day. Stability and calm undergirding and abiding all change.

In summer, there is no snow on the mountain, except perhaps for the very top or in crags shielded from direct sunlight. In the fall, the mountain may display a coat of brilliant fire colors; in winter, a blanket of snow and ice. In any season, it may at times find itself enshrouded in clouds or fog, or pelted by freezing rain. The tourists who come to visit may be disappointed if they can't see the mountain clearly, but it's all the same to the mountain—seen or unseen, in sun or clouds, broiling or frigid, it just sits, being itself. At times visited by violent storms, buffeted by snow and rain and winds of unthinkable magnitude, through it all the mountain sits. Spring comes, the birds sing in the trees once again, leaves return to the trees that lost them, flowers bloom in the high meadows and on the slopes, streams overflow with waters of melting snow. Through it all, the mountain continues to sit, unmoved by the weather, by what happens on the surface, by the world of appearances.

As we sit holding this image in our mind, we can embody the same unwavering stillness and rootedness in the face of everything that changes in our own lives over seconds, hours, and years. In our lives and in our meditation practice, we experience constantly the changing nature of mind and body and of the outer world. We experience periods of light and dark, vivid color and drab dullness. We experience storms of varying intensity and violence in the outer world and in our own lives and minds. Buffeted by high winds, by cold and rain, we endure periods of darkness and pain as well as savor moments of joy and uplift. Even our appearance changes constantly, just like the mountain's, experiencing a weather and a weathering of its own.

By becoming the mountain in our meditation, we can link up with its strength and stability, and adopt them for our own. We can use its energies to support our efforts to encounter each moment with mindfulness, equanimity, and clarity. It may help us to see that our thoughts and feelings, our preoccupations, our emotional storms and crises, even the things that happen to us are much like the weather on the mountain—the result of causes and conditions. We tend to take it personally, but its strongest characteristic is impersonal. The weather of our own lives is not to be ignored or denied. It is to be encountered, honored, felt, known for what it is, and held in high awareness since it can kill us. In holding it in this way, we come to know a deeper silence and stillness and wisdom than we may have thought possible, right within the storms. Mountains have this to teach us, and more, if we can come to listen.

Yet, when all is said and done, the mountain meditation is only a device, a finger pointing us toward somewhere. We still have to look, then go. Although the mountain image can inspire us, and help us become more stable and far-seeing, we human beings are much more interesting and complex than mountains, for all their beauty and complexity, and the stories they have to tell. We are breathing, moving, dancing, loving mountains. We can be simultaneously hard like rock, firm, unmoving, and at the same time soft and gentle and flowing. We have a vast range of potentials at our disposal. We can see and feel. We can know and understand. We can imagine. We can learn; we can grow; we can heal; especially if we learn to listen to the inner harmony of things and hold to the central mountain axis of our being through thick and thin.

*

The birds have vanished into the sky,
and now the last cloud drains away.
We sit together, the mountain and me,
until only the mountain remains.

LI PO

TRY: Keeping this mountain image in mind as you sit in formal meditation. Explore its usefulness in deepening your capacity to dwell in stillness; to sit for longer periods of time in the timeless present; to sit in the face of adversity, and with the various, always changing, weather patterns in the mind, be they storms, drabness, or the clear skies of openhearted wakefulness. Ask yourself what you are learning from your experiments with this practice. Can you see some subtle transformation occurring in your attitude toward things that change in your life? Can you carry the mountain image with you in daily life? Can you see the mountain in others and allow them their own shape and form, each mountain uniquely itself?

The Lake Meditation

The mountain image is only one of many that you may find supports your practice and makes it more vivid and elemental. Images of trees, rivers, clouds, sky can be useful allies as well. The image itself is not fundamental, but it can deepen and expand your view of practice.

Some people find the image of a lake particularly helpful. Because a lake is an expanse of water, the image lends itself to the lying-down posture, although it can be practiced sitting up as well. We know that the water principle is every bit as elemental as rock and that its nature is stronger than rock in the sense that water erodes rock over time, wears it down. Water also has the enchanting quality of receptivity. It parts to allow anything in, then resumes itself. If you hit a mountain or a rock with a hammer, in spite of its hardness, or actually because of it, the rock chips, fragments, breaks apart. But if you hit the ocean or a pond with a hammer, all you get is a rusty hammer. A key virtue of water power reveals itself in this.

To practice using the lake image in your meditation, picture in your mind's eye a lake, a body of water held in a receptive basin by the earth itself. Note in the mind's eye and in your own heart that water likes to pool in low places. It seeks its own level, asks to be contained. The lake you invoke may be deep or shallow, blue or green, muddy or clear. With no wind, the surface of the lake is flat. Mirrorlike, it reflects trees, rocks, sky, and clouds, holds everything in itself momentarily. Wind stirs up waves on the lake, from ripples to chop. Clear reflections disappear. But sunlight may still sparkle in the ripples and dance on the waves in a play of shimmering diamonds. When night comes, it's the moon's turn to dance on the lake, or if the surface is still, to be reflected in it along with the outline of trees and shadows. In winter, the lake may freeze over yet teem with movement and life below.

When you have established a picture of the lake in your mind's eye, allow yourself to become one with the lake as you lie down on your back or sit in meditation, so that your energies are held by your embrace of awareness and by your openness and compassion for yourself in the same way as the lake's waters are held by the embracing, receptive, and accepting basin of the earth herself. Breathing with the lake image moment by moment, feeling its body as your body, inviting your mind and your heart to be open and receptive, to reflect whatever comes near. Experience the moments of complete stillness when both reflection and water are completely clear, and other moments when the surface is disturbed, choppy, stirred up, reflections and depth lost for a time. Through it all, as you rest in awareness, simply noting the play of the various energies of your own mind and heart, the fleeting thoughts and feelings, impulses and reactions that come and go as ripples and waves, noting their effects in the same way you observe the various changing energies at play on the lake: the wind, the waves, the light and shadow and reflections, the colors, the smells.

Do your thoughts and feelings disturb the surface? Is that okay with you? Can you see a rippled or wavy surface as an intimate,

essential aspect of being a lake, of having a surface? Can you identify not only with the surface but with the entire body of the water,
so that you become the stillness below the surface as well, which at
most experiences only gentle undulations, even when the surface is
whipped to frothing?

In the same way, in your meditation practice and in your daily
life, can you identify not only with the content of your thoughts and
feelings but also with the vast unwavering reservoir of awareness
itself residing below the surface of the mind? In the lake meditation, we sit with the intention to hold in awareness and acceptance
all the qualities of mind and body, just as the lake sits held, cradled,
contained by the earth, reflecting sun, moon, stars, trees, rocks,
clouds, sky, birds, light, caressed by the air and wind, which bring
out and highlight its sparkle, its vitality, its essence.

*

In such a day, in September or October, Walden is a perfect
forest mirror, set round with stones as precious to my eye as if
fewer or rarer. Nothing so fair, so pure, and at the same time
so large, as a lake, perchance, lies on the surface of the earth.
Sky water. It needs no fence. Nations come and go without
defiling it. It is a mirror which no stone can crack, whose
quicksilver will never wear off, whose gilding Nature continually repairs; no storms, no dust, can dim its surface ever
fresh;—a mirror in which all impurity presented to it sinks,
swept and dusted by the sun's hazy brush,—this the light

dust-cloth,—which retains no breath that is breathed on it, but sends its own to float as clouds high above its surface, and be reflected in its bosom still.

THOREAU, *Walden*

TRY: Using the lake image to support lying or sitting in stillness, not going anywhere, held and cradled in awareness. Note when the mind reflects; when it is embroiled. Note the calm below the surface. Does this image suggest new ways of carrying yourself in times of turmoil?

Walking Meditation

Peace is every step.

> THICH NHAT HANH, *Peace Is Every Step*

I know people who at one time found it very difficult to sit but got deeply into meditation practice through walking. No matter who you are, you can't sit all the time. And some people just find it virtually impossible to stay seated and mindful with the levels of pain and agitation and anger they feel. But they can walk with it.

In traditional monastic settings, periods of sitting meditation are interspersed with periods of walking meditation. They are the same practice. The walking is just as good as the sitting. What is important is how you keep your mind.

In formal walking meditation, you attend to the walking itself. You can focus on the footfall as a whole; or isolated segments of the motion such as lifting, moving, placing, shifting; or on the whole body moving. You can couple an awareness of walking with an awareness of breathing.

In walking meditation, you are not walking to get anywhere. The invitation—and the challenge—is to see whether it is possible to be where you actually are with each and every step. A common way to practice is simply to walk back and forth in a lane, or round and round in a loop. Literally having no place to go makes it easier to be where you already are. What's the point of trying to be somewhere else on your walking path when it really is all the same? So the challenge is always the same too: Can you be fully with this step, with this breath?

Walking meditation can be practiced at any pace, from ultraslow to very brisk. How much of the foot cycle you can attend to will depend on the speed. The practice is to take each step as it comes and to be fully present with it. This means feeling the very sensations of walking—in your feet, in your legs, in the carriage of the torso and head, in the gait—as always, moment by moment, and in this case, step by step as well. You might call it "watching your step," pun intended, although it is an inner watching. You're not looking at your feet!

Just as in the sitting meditation, things will come up that will pull your attention away from the bare experience of walking. We work with those perceptions, sights, sounds, thoughts, feelings and impulses, memories and anticipations that come up during the walking in the very same way that we do in sitting meditation. Ultimately, walking is stillness in motion, flowing mindfulness.

It's best to practice formal walking meditation in a place where you won't become a spectacle to other people, especially if you are going to do it very slowly. Good places are your living room, fields, or a clearing in the woods; isolated beaches are good, too. Push a shopping cart in front of you through a supermarket, and you can walk as slowly as you like.

You can practice walking meditation informally anywhere. Informal walking meditation doesn't involve pacing back and forth or going around a loop but just walking normally. You can walk mindfully along a sidewalk, down a corridor at work, going for a hike, walking your dog, walking with children. It involves recalling that you are here in your body. You simply remind yourself to be in this moment, taking each step as it comes, accepting each moment as it comes. If you find yourself rushing or becoming impatient, slowing the pace can help take the edge off your rushing and remind you that you are here now, and that when you get there, you will be there. If you miss the here, you are likely also to miss the there. If your mind is not here now, it is likely not to be fully present just because you arrive somewhere else.

TRY: Bringing awareness to walking, wherever you find yourself. Slow it down a bit. Center yourself in your body and in the present moment. Appreciate the fact that you are able to walk, which many people cannot. Perceive how miraculous it is, and for a moment, don't take for granted that your body works so wonderfully. Know that you are ambulating upright on the face of Mother Earth and, simultaneously, within the fragile and not very deep ocean of air enveloping her. As best you can, walk with dignity and confidence. And as the Navajo/Diné blessing offers, may you walk in beauty, wherever you find yourself.

Try walking formally as well. Before or after you sit, try a period of walking meditation. Keep a continuity of mindfulness between the walking and the sitting. Ten minutes is good, or half an hour. Remember once again that it is not clock time we are concerned with here. But you will learn more and understand walking meditation more deeply if you challenge yourself to keep at it past your first or second impulse to stop.

Standing Meditation

Standing meditation is best learned from trees. Stand close to one or, better still, in a stand of trees, and just peer out in one direction. Feel your feet developing roots into the ground. Feel your body sway gently, as it always will, just as trees do in a breeze. Staying put, in touch with your breathing, drink in what is in front of you, or keep your eyes closed and sense your surroundings, the air around the body. Sense the tree closest to you. Listen to it, feel its presence, touch it with your mind and body.

Use your breath to help you to stay in the moment… feeling your own body standing, breathing, being, moment by moment.

When mind or body first signals that perhaps it is time to move on, stay with the standing a while longer, remembering that trees stand still for years, some for centuries, a few for maybe a millennium or more. See if they do not have something to teach you about stillness, about presence, and about being in touch. After all, they are touching the ground with roots and trunk, the air with trunk and branches, air and sunlight with their leaves or needles. Everything about a standing tree speaks of being in touch. Experiment with standing this way yourself, even for short periods of time. Sensing the air on your skin and the feeling of your feet in contact with the ground. Feeling the body being bathed in the sounds of the world and by the play of light, color, and shadow. Sensing the breath moving in and out of the body, and the mind's incessant activity.

It might help to keep in mind that trees breathe in and thereby capture, through their needles or leaves, the carbon dioxide that you and I breathe out. And they breathe out, through their needles or leaves, the oxygen that you and I breathe in. Quite an intertwining of life on the planet, a dynamic that we are putting in graver and graver danger. Keep in mind that the green chlorophyll molecule of the plant kingdom is by far life's major way of capturing energy from the sun and is thus the ultimate source of all our food. And that the cosmos, along with billions of years of evolution here on earth, also came up with the heme in hemoglobin, a fourfold porphyrin ring very similar in structure to the chlorophyll molecule but with an iron atom at its center rather than a magnesium atom and so red, not green. And where did those Mg^{++} and Fe^{++} atoms come from? From the interior of former generations of exploding stars. Quite an interweaving of Big Bang cosmology, stellar evolution, the periodic table of the elements, and our present circumstances on earth—and so worth paying close attention to and appreciating the remarkable interconnectedness in which we are embedded and which underlies everything of which we are made.

May our standing meditation be a deep bow to the trees and to the planet's two major rain forests, the Amazon and the Congo, often referred to as the earth's lungs. May they not disappear out of our ignorance and greed.

TRY: Standing still wherever you find yourself, in the woods, in the mountains, by a river, in your living room, or just waiting for the bus. When you are alone, you might try standing with your palms open to the sky and your arms out in various positions, like branches and leaves, accessible, open, receptive, patient—and at the same time, feeling yourself rooted to the ground, the earth, through your legs and feet—the condensation of everything everywhere that has come together to give us life in this timeless only moment we call now.

Lying-Down Meditation

Lying down is a wonderful way to meditate if you can manage not to fall asleep. And if you do fall asleep, your sleep may be more restful if you enter it through meditation. You can wake up from sleeping in the same way, bringing full awareness to those first moments of wakefulness returning.

When your body is lying down, you can really let the whole of it go much more easily than you can in any other posture. You can intentionally and wholeheartedly surrender to the gravitational pull of Mother Earth. Your body can sink into the bed, mat, floor, or ground until your muscles stop making the slightest effort to hold you together. This is a profound letting go at the level of both your muscles and the motor neurons that govern them. The mind quickly follows if you give it permission to stay open and wakeful.

Using the body as a whole as the object of your attending in lying-down meditations is a veritable blessing. You give yourself over to feeling it from head to toe, breathing and radiating warmth over the entire envelope of your skin. It's the whole body that breathes, the whole body that is alive. In bringing mindfulness to the body as a whole, you reclaim your entire body as the locus of your being and your vitality, and remind yourself that "you," whoever you are, are not just a resident of your head. The body is a universe unto itself, with orders of magnitude more cells, never mind atoms, than the estimated number of galaxies in the observable universe.

You can also focus on different areas of the body in either a free-flowing or a more systematic way when cultivating mindfulness lying down. In MBSR, we introduce people to lying-down meditation in the form of a forty-five-minute body scan. Not everybody can sit for forty-five minutes right away, but pretty much anybody can do the body scan. All you need to do is lie down, even in bed, or on the bed, tune in to and *feel* the different regions of your body as fully as possible in the moment, and then let go of them. The body scan is systematic in the sense that we move through the various regions of the body in a particular order. But there is no one way to do it. It could be done scanning from head to feet or from feet to head or from side to side for that matter. And if you can't manage forty-five minutes, any amount of time is good. The most important thing is your motivation and your willingness to see meditation practice as a radical act of kindness and caring extended toward yourself, body and mind, heart and soul.

One way to practice is to intentionally direct your breath into and out from the various regions of your body, as if you could breathe right in "to" your toes, or a knee, or your ear, and breathe out "from" those places. And after a time, however brief or extended, when you feel ready to, on an outbreath you just let go of whatever region you were focusing on, allowing/inviting it to dissolve in your mind's eye or your imagination as the muscles themselves let go and you drop into stillness and open awareness—before moving on and connecting with the next region of the body, which you would come to on another inbreath. As much as possible, allowing all the breathing to be through your nose.

You don't have to do lying-down meditation as systematically as in the body scan, however. You can also focus on particular regions of your body at will or as they become dominant in the field of your awareness, perhaps due to pain or a problem with a particular region. Entering into them with openness and attention and acceptance can be profoundly healing, especially if you practice regularly. As was said, it can feel like a deep nourishing of cells and tissues as well as of psyche and spirit, body and soul, the totality of your being.

Lying-down meditation is a good way to get in touch with your emotional body, too. We possess a metaphorical, a mythical heart, as well as a physical one. When we focus on the region of the heart, it can be helpful to tune in to any sensations of constriction in the chest, tightness or heaviness, and be aware of emotions such as grief, sadness, fear, loneliness, despair, unworthiness, or anger that may lie just beneath the surface of those physical sensations. We speak of being broken-hearted, hard-hearted, or heavy-hearted because the heart carries a poetic license all its own in our culture as the seat of our emotional life. It is equally the seat of love, joy, and compassion, and such emotions are equally deserving of attention and honoring as you recognize, cultivate, and befriend them.

A number of specialized meditative practices such as loving-kindness meditation are specifically oriented toward cultivating in oneself particular conditions that expand and open the metaphorical heart. Acceptance, forgiveness, lovingkindness, generosity, and trust are all strengthened by intentionally centering and sustaining attention in the heart region and by invoking such feelings as part of formal meditation practice. But these feelings can also be strengthened through simply recognizing them when they arise spontaneously in your meditation practice and in everyday life, and embracing them in awareness.

Other body regions, too, have metaphorical meaning and can be approached in meditations, lying down and otherwise, with this kind of embodied awareness. The solar plexus has a sunlike, radiant quality and can help us to contact feelings of expansiveness. The belly, as the seat of the digestive fires, conveys feelings of vitality, stability, centeredness. The throat vocalizes our emotions and can be either constricted or open. Feelings can get "caught in the throat" sometimes, even if the heart is open. When we develop mindfulness of the throat region, it can put us more in touch with our speech and its tonal qualities—such as explosiveness, speed, harshness, volume, automaticity on the one hand, or softness, gentleness, sensitivity on the other—as well as its content. Attention to this region over time can help us to locate or reclaim our authentic voice.

Similarly, each region of the physical body has its counterpart in an emotional body or map that carries a deeper meaning for us, often completely below our level of awareness. In order to continue growing across the life span, it is helpful to activate, listen to, and learn from our emotional body. Lying-down meditations can help a lot with this as long as when you get up, you are willing to risk taking the stands that your insights might require. In the old days, our cultures, mythologies, and rituals helped in the process of activating our emotional body and honoring its vitality and its impermanence. Usually this was done through traditional initiation practices organized by the community of elders, whose job it was to educate the adolescents about what it meant to be a full-fledged adult within the tribe or culture. The importance of the development of the emotional body is hardly recognized today. We are pretty much left to our own devices to come to full adulthood, however we identify, unless we can find others like us with whom to connect in community. Given the speed at which society is changing, there may no longer be any agreed-upon collective knowledge of how to guide the awakening emotional vitality and authenticity of our young people, our children, especially now that social media and its algorithm-driven toxicity dominates the mindscapes of so many. Mindfulness, in all its diversity, inclusivity, and openhearted spaciousness, and its increasingly widespread introduction into schools along with social-emotional learning curricula, may contribute to a reawakening of fundamental human values such as kindness and compassion, empathy and non-harming in young people and in future generations.

Since we lie down for so much of our lives, we have many occasions in which lying-down meditations can provide readily accessible gateways to moments of mindfulness. Whether it be before sleep, while resting or just lounging around, or upon waking in the morning, the lying down itself can provide both an opportunity and an easy glidepath into the practice of mindfulness, filling your body, at least momentarily, with awareness, equanimity, and acceptance of things as they are in the present moment. These mind moments can be accessed simply by dropping into the body and the breath momentarily, just listening, listening, hearing, hearing, feeling, feeling, settling into the moment, letting go, letting be, and simply resting in awareness, outside of time...

And possibly most beneficial of all, when you wake up in the morning, instead of jumping out of bed on autopilot and perhaps feeling you are "already late," why not wake up a bit earlier for the express purpose of leaving some time for tuning in to the body lying in bed breathing and feeling what is here to be felt in whatever format or form seems most congenial to you in that moment? In other words, why not devote a few minutes at least to making sure you are really awake before launching yourself out of bed and into the day? Might that not invite your entire day to become more of a seamless unfolding of the meditation practice? And thus lead to perhaps having more of your *doing* that day come out of *being*? A stretch of meditating in bed in the morning is akin to a musician carefully tuning their instrument before taking it out on the road and playing it in public. It just might feed forward and influence the quality of your moments throughout the day.

TRY: Tuning in to your breath when you find yourself lying down, on your back if possible, in what is traditionally called the *corpse pose* in yoga.* Feel the breath moving in your belly and in your entire body. Dwell with the breath in various regions such as

---

* See my "Dying Before You Die—Deux," in *The Healing Power of Mindfulness: A New Way of Being*, Hachette, New York, 2018, 205–207.

the feet, the legs, the pelvis and genitals, the belly, the chest, the back, the shoulders, the arms, the throat and neck, the head, the face, the top of your head—tuning in and listening carefully, allowing yourself to feel whatever is present. Watch the sensations in the body flux and change. Watch your feelings about them flux and change.

Try meditating on purpose lying down, not just around bedtime. Do it out of bed, on the floor, at different times of the day. Do it in fields and meadows on occasion, under trees, in the rain, in the snow.

Bring particular attention to your body as you are going to sleep and especially as you are waking up. Even for a few minutes, stretch yourself out straight, on your back if possible, and just feel the body as a whole breathing. Give special attention to any regions that are problematic for you, and work at letting the breath invite them back into a sense of membership and wholeness with the rest of your body. Keep your emotional body in mind. Honor "gut" feelings.

Getting Your Body Down on the Floor at Least Once a Day

There is a particular feeling of time stopping when you get your body down on the floor, whether it's to practice a lying-down meditation such as the body scan or to systematically work the body gently but firmly toward its limits in first this direction, then that, as we do in mindful hatha yoga. Just being low down in a room tends to clear the mind. Maybe it's because being on the floor is so foreign to us that it breaks up our habitual neurological patterning and invites us to enter into this moment through a sudden opening in what we might call the body door.

In mindful hatha yoga practice, the idea is to be fully in your body as you bring awareness to the various sensations, thoughts, and feelings that come up while you are moving, stretching, breathing, balancing, holding positions, reaching or lifting with arms, legs, torso, and head. There are said to be more than eighty thousand basic yoga postures, and at least ten variants of each. One won't quickly run out of new challenges for the body, but I find I keep coming back to a core routine of maybe twenty or so postures, which over the decades, starting in my twenties, just keep taking me deeper into my body and deeper into stillness and wellbeing.

Yoga folds movement and stillness into one another, leavened by present-moment awareness. It is a wonderfully nourishing practice.

As with other mindfulness practices, you are not trying to get anywhere. But you are purposefully moving right up to the very limits of your body in this moment to investigate with both interest and kindness where those limits lie and how it feels to dwell this side of them. You are exploring a terrain where there may be considerable intensity of sensation associated with stretching or lifting or maintaining your balance in unusual spatial configurations of limbs, head, and trunk. And there you dwell, usually for longer than part of your mind would like, just breathing, just feeling your body, not forcing anything at all, just lovingly exploring how things are. You are not looking to break through to anything. You are not competing with anybody else's body or even aiming to improve your own. You are not judging how your body is doing. You are simply residing in stillness, within the full range of your experiences, including any intensity or discomfort (which should in any case be benign if you have not forced yourself to go beyond your limits), tasting the bloom of these moments in your body.

All the same, for the devoted practitioner, it's hard not to notice that the body loves a steady diet of this and changes on its own over time. There is frequently an "on the way to" quality to this practice at the same time that there is the "just as it is now" feeling as the body sinks more and more deeply into a stretch or into letting go, lying on the floor between more effortful postures. Not forcing anything, we just do our best to line up with the warp and woof of body and mind, floor, world, and moment, staying in exquisite touch with how things are.

TRY: Getting down on the floor once a day and working with your body as you find it, stretching within the limits that reveal themselves as you engage with it, moving ever so gently and attentively, if only for three or four minutes at first. Stay in touch with your breathing and with what your body is telling you. Remind yourself that this is your body today. Check to see whether you are in touch with it. And how do you do that? Awareness. It is that simple—and profound—and enlivening.

Not Practicing Is Practicing

Sometimes I like to point out that not doing yoga is the same as doing yoga, although I hope people don't get the wrong idea and think I am saying it's the same whether you practice or not. What I mean is simply that every time you come back to mindful yoga practice, you see the effect of not having done it for a while. So in a way, you learn more by coming back to it than you would by just keeping it up.

Of course, this is only true if you notice things such as how still your body feels, how hard it is to hold a posture, how impatient the mind becomes, how it resists staying on the breath. These things are really hard not to notice when you are down on the floor holding on to your leg behind your knee as you draw your head up toward it. They are much harder to be aware of when it's life itself that we are talking about rather than yoga. But the same principle applies. Yoga and life are different ways of saying the same thing. Forgetting or neglecting to be mindful can teach you a lot more than just being mindful all the time. Fortunately, most of us don't have to worry on that score, since our tendencies toward mindlessness are so robust. It is in the coming back to mindfulness that seeing lies.

TRY: Noticing the difference in how you feel and how you handle stress in periods when you are into the discipline of daily meditation and yoga practice and in periods of your life when you are not. See whether you can become aware of the consequences of your more mindless and automatic behaviors, especially when they are provoked by pressures stemming from work or home life. How do you carry yourself in your body in those periods when you are practicing and when you are not? What happens to your commitment to remember non-doing? How does the lack of regular practice affect your anxiety about time and about achieving certain results? How does it affect your relationships? Where do some of your most mindless patterns come from? What triggers them? Are you ready to hold them in awareness as they grip you by the throat, whether your formal practice is strong this week or not? Can you see that *not* practicing mindfulness is its own arduous practice—with its own built-in sequelae?

Lovingkindness Meditation

No man is an Island, entire of itself;

Every man is a piece of the continent, a part of the main;

If a clod be washed away by the sea,

Europe is the less, as well as if a promontory were,

As well as if a manor of thy friends or of thine own were;

Any man's death diminishes me, because I am involved in mankind;

And therefore, never send to know for whom the bell tolls;

It tolls for thee.

JOHN DONNE, *Meditation XVII*

We resonate with one another's sorrows because we are interconnected. Being whole and simultaneously part of larger and larger spheres of wholeness, we change the world simply by changing ourselves. If I become a center of love and kindness in this moment, then in a perhaps small but hardly insignificant way, the world now has a nucleus of love and kindness it lacked the moment before. This benefits me and it benefits others.

You may have noticed that you are not always a center of love and kindness, even toward yourself. In fact, in our society, one might speak of an epidemic of depression, loneliness, and low self-esteem. This is not new, but it is getting increasingly pervasive. The mean age of onset of major depression has come down lower and lower over the past century. Depression, dysmorphia, and other expressions of self-loathing and lack of self-worth are now pervasive among teenagers. Decades ago now, in conversations with the Dalai Lama during a Mind and Life meeting in Dharamsala in 1990, he did a double take when a Western psychologist spoke of low self-esteem in the United States. The phrase had to be translated into Tibetan for him several times, although his English is quite good. He just couldn't grasp the notion of low self-esteem, and when he finally understood what was being said, he was visibly saddened to hear that so many people in America carry deep feelings of self-loathing and inadequacy, only compounded in the subsequent decades. Now, driven by social media and other factors, it has become a public mental health crisis of epidemic proportions, especially among the young.

At the time of that conversation, such feelings were virtually unheard of among the Tibetans. They had all the severe problems of refugees from oppression living in the Third World, but low self-esteem was not one of them. Who knows what will happen to future generations as they come into contact with what we ironically call the "developed world"? Maybe we are overdeveloped outwardly and underdeveloped inwardly. Perhaps it is we who, for all our wealth, are living in poverty.

You can take steps to rectify this poverty through lovingkindness meditation. As usual, the place to begin is with yourself. Might it be possible for you to invite a sense of kindness and acceptance and an embracing of your own beauty and worthiness as a human being to arise in your heart right now? As a systematic practice, of course, you would have to do so over and over again, in the same way you would exercise a muscle, working *with* whatever resistance arises, in this case bringing your mind back to the breath sensations in the body over and over again as in the sitting meditation practice. The mind won't take easily to it, because the wounds we carry run deep. But you might try, just as an experiment, to hold yourself in awareness for a time in your formal meditation practice as a mother or father would hold a hurt or frightened child, with total acceptance and unconditional love. Might it be possible for you to cultivate that tenderness for yourself, even for brief moments, right here, right now? Can you intentionally experiment with forgiving yourself, if not others, right here, right now? Is it even possible to invite yourself to be at home in this moment in your body, in your own skin, in your heart, with things exactly as they are? Might it actually be okay for you to feel okay in this moment? Is there any basis for well-being and happiness to be present for you in this moment at all?

The formal practice of lovingkindness can be embarked on in the following way. But please don't mistake the words for the practice. As usual, they are just signposts pointing the way:

Start by settling yourself into whatever posture you adopt, presumably one embodying wakefulness and dignity, anchored in the sensations of the body breathing. Then, from your heart or from your belly, invite feelings or images of kindness and love to radiate, sunlike, in all directions, until they fill your whole being. Allow yourself to be cradled by your own awareness as if you were as deserving of lovingkindness as any child. Let your awareness embody benevolent mother energy, or benevolent father energy, or benevolent friend energy, making available for you in this moment a recognition and an honoring of your own being, and a kindness and unconditional acceptance you perhaps did not receive enough of, if any, as a child. Let yourself bask in this energy of loving-kindness, breathing it in and breathing it out as if it were an oxygen line straight into your heart, a lifeline, long in disrepair, but finally passing along a vital nourishment you may have been sorely lacking, perhaps without even knowing it consciously, for a long, long time.

If you care to, you might play with inviting feelings of kindness and unconditional acceptance to arise and fill your heart, maybe recalling a time when you yourself felt totally seen and accepted by someone who saw you for who you always were, in your fullness, in your original beauty. Can you tap into those feelings right here and right now, in your body, in your mind, in your heart?

Some people find it valuable to say to themselves from time to time, or even out loud, such things as, "May I be free from ignorance." "May I be free from self-centeredness." "May I be free from greed and hatred." "May I not suffer." "May I be happy." After each voicing, just let your experience be what it is in the moment, unattached to attaining any particular feeling or result. The words and phrases are simply invitational, offered to recall, evoke, and nurture feelings of lovingkindness that may arise spontaneously when invited. They serve as consciously formed intentions to be free now, in this timeless moment at least, from the problems we so often make for ourselves or compound through our own fear and forgetfulness, from our habit of losing touch with our own intrinsic beauty and worthiness.

Once you have established yourself as a luminous center radiating love and kindness throughout your being—which amounts to a cradling and enveloping of yourself in lovingkindness and acceptance—you can dwell here indefinitely, drinking at this fount, bathing in it, renewing yourself, nourishing yourself, enlivening yourself. This can be a profoundly healing practice on every level of your being.

You can also take the practice further. Having established a warm center of lovingkindness in your body and in your heart, you can let its energies radiate outwardly in all directions to benefit the entire world or direct those energies more specifically wherever you care to. You might experiment with directing lovingkindness toward the members of your immediate family, biological and/or chosen. If you have children, you might experiment with holding them in your heart and in your mind's eye, visualizing their essential selves, wishing them well . . . saying to yourself inwardly, "May they not suffer, may they come to know their true way in the world, may they experience love and acceptance and belonging." And then, as you care to, expanding the field of lovingkindness to include, as you go along, a partner, spouse, siblings, parents, your children's children...

You can direct lovingkindness toward your parents whether they are alive or dead, wishing them well, wishing that they may not feel isolated or in pain, honoring them. If you feel capable of it and it feels healthy to you, and liberating, seeing if you can find a place in your heart to forgive them for their limitations, for their fears, and for any wrong actions and suffering they may have caused, remembering Yeats's line, "Why, what could she have done, being what she is?"

And there's no need to stop here. You can direct lovingkindness toward anybody, toward people you know and people you don't. Toward your ancestors, known and unknown, a chain of individuals going back in time endlessly, whose lives somehow mysteriously resulted in your life in this moment. A practice of this kind may or may not benefit those who are still living, but it will certainly benefit you by refining and extending your emotional being. This extension matures as you purposefully direct lovingkindness toward people in the present that you have a hard time with, toward those you dislike or have an aversion for, toward those whom you find threatening or who have hurt you. You can also practice directing lovingkindness toward whole groups of people—toward all those in a community or on the planet who are oppressed, or who suffer, or whose lives are caught up in war or violence or hatred, understanding that they are not different from you— that they too have loved ones; hopes and aspirations; need for shelter, food, and peace. You can also extend lovingkindness to the planet itself, to its glories and to its suffering, to the biosphere and the planetary cycles that support it, sometimes called Gaia, the living earth that we are wittingly and unwittingly despoiling. Can we direct lovingkindness to the streams and rivers, to the air, the oceans, the forests, to plants and animals, collectively or singly?

There is really no natural limit to the practice of lovingkindness in meditation or in one's life. It is an ongoing, ever-expanding realization and honoring of interconnectedness. It is also its living embodiment. When you can love one tree or one flower or one dog or one place or one person or yourself for one moment, you can find all people, all places, all suffering, all harmony in that one moment. Practicing in this way is not trying to change anything or get anywhere, although it might look like it on the surface. What it is really doing is uncovering what is and always has been already present. Love and kindness are here all the time, somewhere, in fact, everywhere. Usually our ability to touch them and be touched by them lies buried beneath our own fears and hurts, underneath our own self-privileging tendencies toward greed and hatred, beneath our desperate clinging to the illusion that we are separate and alone.

By intentionally invoking such feelings and inviting them into our practice, we are stretching into, and thereby recognizing, the edges of our own ignorance, just as in the mindful yoga practice, we work with and stretch into the resistance of muscle, ligament, and tendon and, as in that and all other forms of meditation practice, come to recognize and watch dissolve the artificial boundaries, delusions, and ignorance imprisoning our minds and hearts. And in the stretching, painful as it sometimes is, we ourselves benefit. We expand, we grow. To at least a degree, we are liberated from ignorance and delusion, from the dominance of greed and hatred, from the selfing impulse. As we change ourselves, in perhaps tiny but hardly insignificant ways, we change the world, just as the properties of a mono-crystal lattice structure are profoundly changed in useful ways by a subtle seeding with a dose of other atoms, as we have already seen. In the brain, mounting evidence suggests that important changes in what is called functional connectivity, where different brain regions begin talking to each other in new ways, are driven by regular meditation practice.

So, in very real and hardly insignificant ways, when we change ourselves, we have already begun to change the world.

*

My religion is kindness.

THE DALAI LAMA

TRY: Touching base with feelings of lovingkindness within yourself at some point in your meditation practice. Try it on a regular basis, maybe at the end of a period of sitting or after practicing the body scan. See whether you can get behind any objections you may have to developing this particular practice or behind any reasons you might conjure up for being in some way unlovable or unworthy. Try looking at all that as mere thinking, which it is, rather than the truth of anything. Experiment with allowing yourself to bathe in the warmth and acceptance of lovingkindness as if you were a child held in a loving mother's or father's arms. Then play with directing it toward others and letting it radiate out on its own into the world. There is no limit to this practice, but as with any other practice, it deepens and grows with constant tending, like plants in a tenderly cared-for garden. Make sure that as you practice, you are not trying in that moment to help anybody else or even the planet. Rather, you are simply holding whoever it is in awareness, honoring them, wishing them well, opening to their pain and suffering with kindness and compassion and acceptance.

If, in the process, you find that this practice of lovingkindness calls you to act differently in the world, then by all means, act—the wellbeing of the world depends on it—and let those actions too embody lovingkindness and mindfulness.

PART THREE

In the Spirit of Mindfulness

All of us are apprenticed to the same teacher that the religious institutions originally worked with: reality. Reality-insight says...master the twenty-four hours. Do it well, without self-pity. It is as hard to get the children herded into the car pool and down the road to the bus as it is to chant sutras in the Buddha-hall on a cold morning. One move is not better than the other, each can be quite boring, and they both have the virtuous quality of repetition. Repetition and ritual and their good results come in many forms. Changing the filter, wiping noses, going to meetings, picking up around the house, washing dishes, checking the dipstick—don't let yourself think these are distracting you from your more serious pursuits. Such a round of chores is not a set of difficulties we hope to escape from so that we may do our "practice" which will put us on a "path"—it is our path.

GARY SNYDER, *The Practice of the Wild*

Sitting by Fire

In the old days, once the sun went down, the only source of light people had, other than the changing moon and the firmament of stars, planets, and various celestial objects, was fire. For millions of years, we human beings sat around fires, gazing into the flames and embers with cold and darkness at our backs. Maybe this is where formal meditation got its start.

Fire was a comfort to us, our source of heat, light, and protection—dangerous but, with great care, controllable. Sitting by it gave us a sense of ease and security at the end of the day. In its warm, flickering light, we could relax, tell stories, talk about the day past, sing, or just sit silently, seeing the reflection of our minds in the ever-changing flames and the glowing ember landscapes of a magical world. Fire made the darkness bearable and helped us feel secure and safe. It was calming, reliable, restoring, meditative, and absolutely necessary for survival.

This necessity has flown from our everyday lives, and with it almost all occasion to be still and rest in non-doing, in a secure and timeless stillness. In today's fast-paced world, fires are impractical or an occasional luxury to set a certain mood. We have only to flip a switch when the outer light begins to dim. We can light up the world as brightly as we want and keep going with our lives, filling all our waking hours with busyness, with doing, with perpetual self-distraction. Life affords us scant time for being nowadays, unless we seize the opportunity on purpose. We no longer have a fixed time when we have to stop everything we are doing because there's simply too little light to do it by. As a consequence, we lack that formerly built-in time we had every night for shifting gears, for letting go of the day's activities. We have precious few occasions nowadays for the mind to settle itself in stillness by a fire.

Instead, we easily get lost in screens, big screens, little screens, all day long at work for many of us and for even more of us, at day's end. These are all pale electronic fire, and it pales in comparison to the real thing. We submit ourselves to constant bombardment by images and sounds that come from minds other than our own, filling our heads with information and trivia, with other people's adventures, opinions, excitements, and desires. Watching endlessly growing television outlets, or mindlessly wandering the well-named warren of infinite digital rabbit holes, leaves even less room in the day for experiencing stillness and the domain of being. The pale addictive fire soaks up time, space, and silence, a soporific lulling us into mindless passivity.

Meanwhile, life unfolds, our moments go by. At one point, many decades ago, people started calling television "chewing gum for the eyes." Now exponentially compounded by the digital revolution, by an invisible but not benign surveillance capitalism underlying every click of a device online, by an ever-more-seductive and ubiquitous attention economy, by social media echo chambers divorced from facts and reality and driven by algorithms optimizing screen time and "engagement," to say nothing of chatbots, artificial intelligence (AI), and the promise of infinite creativity (and the potential apocalyptic specter of new generations of ever-"smarter" thinking machines) at all our fingertips and soon, intangible interfaces, things have only gotten more seductive, dangerous, dysregulated, and dystopian. At the same time, the whole of it is ever harder to apprehend and comprehend its effects on us, including on young developing minds. Perhaps it would be good to realize, in the sense of "make real," the full dimensionality of our analog genius as a species, before we lose it completely to our increasingly addictive digital precocity.

A free press is critical to democracy. Yet even newspapers, now increasingly in digital form, can also rob us of precious moments in which we might be living more fully. How informed do we actually have to be? And are we being informed about the most important things or living lives of perpetual absorption and self-distraction?

Of course, we don't have to succumb to the addictive appeals of external absorptions in entertainment and passionate distractions. We can touch base with and even anchor ourselves in our own unique agency and exercise a degree of sovereignty over ourselves and our twenty-four hours. We can develop other ways of being and adopt practices that bring us back to that elemental yearning inside ourselves for warmth, stillness, connection, peacefulness, wellbeing, and the radical ease of non-doing. When we sit with our breathing, for instance, it is much like sitting by fire. Looking deeply into the breath, we can see, at least as much as in glowing coals and embers and flames, reflections of our own mind dancing. A certain warmth is generated, too. And if we are truly not trying to get anywhere but simply allow ourselves to be here in this timeless moment as it is, we can stumble easily upon an ancient stillness and sense of absolute belonging—behind and within the play of our thoughts and feelings and busy lives—that in a simpler time, people found in sitting by the fire.

Harmony—and Its Fleetingness

As I pull into the parking lot of the hospital, several hundred geese pass overhead. They are flying high, and I do not hear their honking. What strikes me first is that they clearly know where they are going. They are flying in a northwesterly direction, and there are so many of them that the curving formation trails out far to the east, where the early November sun is hugging the horizon. As the first of them fly over, I am moved by the nobility and beauty of their purposeful assembly in the air to grab paper and pen right there in the car and attempt to capture the pattern as best my unskilled hand and eye are able. Rapid strokes suffice... they will shortly be gone.

Hundreds are in Vs, but many are in more complex arrangements. Everything is in motion. Their lines dip and ascend with grace and harmony, like silk streamers waving in the air. It is clear that they are in touch with each other, communicating. Each somehow knows where it is in the formation, belongs, has its place in this complex and constantly changing pattern.

I feel strangely blessed by their passage. This moment is a gift. I have been permitted to see and share in something I know is important, something I am not graced with that often. Part of it is their wildness, part is the harmony, order, and beauty they embody. Their belonging invites a sensing of my own.

My usual experience of time flowing is suspended while witnessing their passing. The pattern is what scientists call "chaotic," fractal, like cloud formations or the shapes of trees. There is order and, within it, embedded disorder, yet that too is orderly. For me now, it is simply the gift of wonder and amazement. Nature is showing me as I arrive at work today how things actually are in one small sphere, reminding me how little we humans know, and how little we appreciate harmony, or even see it.

And so, reading the newspaper that evening, I note that the full consequences of logging the rain forests covering the high ground in the South Philippines were not apparent until a typhoon struck, and the denuded earth, no longer able to hold water, let it rush unchecked to the lowlands at four times the usual volume and drowned thousands of poor inhabitants of the region. As the popular bumper sticker says, "Shit happens." The trouble is, too often we are unwilling to see our role in it. There are definite risks to disdaining the harmony of things.

Nature's harmony is around us and within us at all times. Perceiving it is an occasion for spontaneous gladness and a sense of wellbeing, but it is often only appreciated in retrospect or in its absence. If all is going well in the body, it tends to go unnoticed. Your lack of a headache is not front-page news for your cerebral cortex. Abilities such as walking, seeing, thinking, breathing, and peeing take care of themselves when they do, and so blend into the landscape of automaticity and unawareness, until with misfortune or advancing age, they may not. Unremitting pain, or fear, or loss wakes us up to the law of impermanence inexorably at work and brings things into a sometimes stark focus. But by then the harmony is harder to see, and we find ourselves caught up in turbulence, itself containing, like rapids and waterfalls, order of a more difficult and subtle level within the river of life. As Joni Mitchell sings, "You don't know what you've got till it's gone..."

As I get out of the car, I inwardly bow to these wayfarers for anointing the airspace of this necessarily civilized hospital parking lot with a refreshing dose of natural wildness.

TRY: Drawing back the veil of unawareness to perceive harmony in this moment. Can you see it in clouds, in sky, in people, in the weather, in food, in your body, in this breath? Look, and look again, right here, right now!

Early Morning

Even though he had no job to go to, no children to feed and get off to school, no external reasons to get up early, it was Thoreau's custom, for the time he lived at Walden, to wake early in the morning and bathe in the pond at dawn. He did it for inner reasons, as a spiritual discipline in itself: "It was a religious exercise, and one of the best things I did."

Benjamin Franklin also extolled the virtues of health, wealth, and wisdom obtained from waking up early in his well-known adage on the subject. But he didn't just mouth it; he practiced it.

The virtues of getting up early have nothing to do with cramming more hours of busyness and accomplishment into one's day. Just the opposite. They stem from the stillness and solitude of the hour, and the potential to use that time to cultivate increasing intimacy with awareness itself. With wise intention, it can be a time for embodied wakefulness, with no agenda other than to be fully present. It then becomes a time outside of time, a moment for simply being. The peacefulness, the darkness, the dawn, the stillness, the solitude—all contribute to making early morning a special time for mindfulness practice.

Waking early has the added value of giving you a very real head start on the day. If you can begin your day with a firm foundation in mindfulness and inner wellbeing, then when you do have to start in on all the doing, it is much more likely that that doing will flow out of your being. You are much more likely to be anchored in mindfulness rather than in mindlessness. You are much more likely to effortlessly carry an inner calmness and balance of mind with you throughout the day—or more easily recover it—than had you just jumped out of bed on autopilot and reflexively started in on the demands and responsibilities of the day, however pressing and important.

The power of waking up early in the morning is so great that it can have a profound effect on a person's life, even without a formal meditation practice. Just witnessing the dawn each day is a wake-up call in itself.

But I find early morning a wondrous time for formal medita-tion. No one else is up. The world's rush hasn't launched itself yet. I get out of bed and usually devote about an hour to being, without doing anything. After almost sixty years, it hasn't lost its allure. On occasion it is difficult to wake up and either my mind or my body resists. But part of the value is in doing it anyway, even if I don't feel like it.

One of the principal virtues of a daily discipline is an acquired transparency toward the appeals of transitory mood states. A com-mitment to getting up early to meditate and take your seat in one way or another, literally, becomes independent of wanting or not wanting to do so on any particular morning. The practice calls us to a higher standard—that of remembering the importance of wakefulness and the ease with which we can slip into a pattern of automatic living that lacks awareness and sensitivity. Just wak-ing up early to practice non-doing is itself a tempering process.

Metaphorically speaking, over time, with some consistency and discipline, it generates enough heat to rearrange the very atoms of our being, giving us a new and stronger crystalline lattice structure of mind and body, a lattice structure that keeps us honest, stable, and flexible, and reminds us that there is far more to life than getting things done, even great things.

A reliable discipline that you stick with through thick and thin can provide a constancy that is independent of what kind of a day you had yesterday and what kind of a day you anticipate today. I especially try to make time for formal practice, if just for a few minutes, on days when momentous events happen, happy or distressing, when my mind and the circumstances are in turmoil, when there is lots to be done and feelings are running strong. In this way, I am less likely to miss the inner meaning and opportunities and blessings of such moments, and I might even navigate through them a bit better as a consequence.

By grounding yourself in mindfulness early in the morning, you are reminding yourself that things are always changing, that good and bad things come and go, and that it is possible to embody a perspective of constancy, wisdom, and wellbeing as you face any conditions that present themselves. Making the daily choice to wake up early to practice is an embodiment of this perspective. I sometimes speak of it as my "routine," but it is far from routine. Mindfulness is the very opposite of routine.

If you are reluctant to get up an hour earlier than you ordinarily might, you can always try half an hour, or fifteen minutes, or even five minutes. It's the spirit that counts. As we saw in the chapter

on lying-down meditation, even five minutes of mindfulness practice in bed after you wake up in the morning—or out of bed—can
make a huge difference. And maybe even five minutes of sacrificed
sleep in the moment you are deciding whether to really wake up
will put you in touch with just how attached we are to sleep, and
therefore how much discipline and resolve are required to carve
out even that little time for ourselves to dwell in awareness without doing anything. After all, the thinking mind in that moment
always has the very credible-sounding excuse that because you will
not be accomplishing anything and there's no real pressure to do
it this morning—and perhaps even real reasons not to—why not
catch the extra sleep, which you know you need now, and start
tomorrow?

To overcome such totally predictable opposition from other cor-
ners of the mind, you need to decide the night before that you are
going to wake up, no matter what your thinking comes up with,
and as soon as possible, get on a meditation cushion, bench, or
chair. This is the flavor of true intentionality and inner discipline.
You do it simply because you committed yourself to do it, and you
do it at the appointed time, whether part of the mind feels like it
or not. After a while, the discipline becomes a part of you. It's simply the new way you choose to live. It is not a "should"; it doesn't
involve forcing yourself. Your values and your actions have simply
shifted.

If you are not ready for that yet (or even if you are), you can
always use the very moment of waking up, no matter what time it
comes, as a moment of mindfulness, the very first of the new day.

Before you even move, try getting in touch with the fact that your breath is moving. Feel your body lying in bed. Straighten it out. Ask yourself, "Am I awake now? Do I know that the gift of a new day is being given to me? Will I be awake for it? What will happen today? Right now, I don't really know. Even as I think about what I have to do, can I be open to this not-knowing? Can I see today as an adventure? Can I see right now as filled with possibilities?"

And if you are really daring, and committed, you can also meditate in bed, lying down, preferably stretched out on your back in the corpse pose, as we saw in the chapter on lying-down meditation. Because you just woke up, before you jump out of bed, why not check and see whether you are indeed fully awake, or already lost in thought, or anxious about the day? We say we have woken up, but have we really? Why not finish the job, right here and right now, before our feet even hit the floor? Even a few minutes of formal practice can prime the entire day so that it unfolds with greater embodied awareness.

*

Morning is when I am awake and there is a dawn in me.... We must learn to reawaken and keep ourselves awake, not by mechanical aids, but by an infinite expectation of the dawn, which does not forsake us in our soundest sleep.... To affect the quality of the day, that is the highest of arts.

THOREAU, *Walden*

TRY: Making a commitment to yourself to get up earlier than you otherwise might. Just doing it changes your life. Let that time, whatever its length, be a time of being, a time for intentional wakefulness. You don't want to fill this time with anything other than awareness. No need to go over the day's commitments in your head and live "ahead" of yourself. This is a time of no-time, of stillness, of presence, of being with yourself. Do not check your phone, but do notice the impulse to do so if it arises.

Also, at the moment of waking up, before getting out of bed, get in touch with your breath, feel the various sensations in your body, note any thoughts and feelings that may be present, let mindfulness touch this moment. Can you feel your breathing? Can you perceive the dawning of each inbreath? Can you enjoy the feeling of the breath freely entering your body in this moment? Can you put your mind in your hands, in your feet, in your heart, and feel what is here to be felt in this moment? Ask yourself, "Am I awake now?" Then check and see. And let whatever arises be good enough for now.

Direct Contact

We all carry around ideas and images of reality, frequently garnered from other people or from courses we have taken, books we have read, or from the web, television, radio, newspapers, the culture in general, all of which give us impressions and pictures of how things are and what is occurring. Large language models (LLMs), chatbots, and ever-increasing attempts at artificial general intelligence (AGI) are entering the mix as I write. As a result, we often see things through our thoughts, or someone else's, or through machine-generated outputs, instead of apprehending directly what is right in front of us or within us. Often, we don't even bother to look or check how we feel because we think we already know and understand. As a consequence, we may be closed off to the wonder and vitality of fresh encounters, which are everywhere. And if we are not careful, we can even forget that direct unfiltered contact is even possible. We may lose touch with what is basic and wondrous in our everyday lives and moments and not even know it. We can live inside a dream reality of our own making without even a sense of the loss, the gulf, the unnecessary distance we place between ourselves and experience. Not knowing this, we can be all the more impoverished, spiritually and emotionally. But something wonderful and unique can occur when our contact with the world becomes direct.

Viki Weisskopf, a mentor of mine and friend from long ago, a renowned theoretical physicist at MIT who served for a time as the head of CERN, the European Organization for Nuclear Research, recounted the following poignant story about direct contact:

Several years ago I received an invitation to give a series of lectures at the University of Arizona at Tucson. I was delighted to accept because it would give me a chance to visit the Kitts Peak astronomical observatory, which had a very powerful telescope I had always wanted to look through. I asked my hosts to arrange an evening to visit the observatory so I could look directly at some interesting objects through the telescope. But I was told this would be impossible because the telescope was constantly in use for photography and other research activities. There was no time for simply looking at objects. In that case, I replied, I would not be able to come to deliver my talks. Within days I was informed that everything had been arranged according to my wishes. We drove up the mountain on a wonderfully clear night. The stars and the Milky Way glistened intensely and seemed almost close enough to touch. I entered the cupola and told the technicians who ran the computer-activated telescope that I wanted to see Saturn and a number of the galaxies. It was a great pleasure to observe with my own eyes and with the utmost clarity all the details I had only seen in photographs before. As I looked at all that, I realized that the room had begun to fill with people, and one by one they too peeked into the tele-scope. I was told that these were astronomers attached to the observatory, but they had never before had the opportunity of looking directly at the objects of their investigations. I can only hope that this encounter made them realize the impor-tance of such direct contacts.

VICTOR WEISSKOPF, *The Joy of Insight*

TRY: Looking at your life as at least as interesting and miracu-lous as the moon, the planets, or the stars. What is it that stands between you and direct contact with your own life? What can you do to change that?

Is There Anything Else You Would Like to Tell Me?

Of course, direct contact is hardly inconsequential in the doctor-patient relationship. In fact, an empathic, openhearted presence is hugely helpful in what is often called the clinical encounter. We go to great lengths to help medical students understand the topology of this landscape and not run away from it in terror because it involves their own feelings as individuals and the need to really listen empathically, treating patients as people rather than solely as disease puzzles and opportunities to exercise judgment and control on which they will be graded. So many things can get in the way of direct contact. Many doctors lack formal training in this dimension of medicine. They remain unaware of the crucial importance of effective communication and caring in what we call health care but too often is just disease care, and even good disease care can be sorely lacking if the subject is, or feels, excluded from the equation.

My elderly mother, who lived to be 101, exasperated at her inability to find a doctor willing to treat her concerns seriously, described how, at a follow-up visit initiated by her because she was still not walking well and was in a lot of pain, the orthopedic surgeon who had replaced her hip with an artificial one studied the X-ray, commenting how good it looked ("superb" was the word he used), and didn't make any attempt to examine her real, in-the-flesh hip and leg or to even acknowledge her complaint until she had insisted on it several times. And then, it held little weight—the X-ray was enough to convince him that she shouldn't be having any pain—except she was.

Doctors can unknowingly hide behind their handiwork, their instruments, medical tests, and technical vocabulary, even their busyness. They may be reluctant to come into too direct contact with the patient as a whole person, an individual with unique thoughts and fears, values, cares, and questions, spoken and unspoken. They often doubt their own capacity to do this because it is such uncharted and potentially frightening territory. In part it may be that they are unaccustomed to looking at their own thoughts and fears, values, cares, and doubts, so someone else's can feel pretty intimidating. And it may be that they don't feel they have time to open these potential floodgates, or that they doubt they would know how to respond adequately. But what is required most by patients is simply listening, being present, taking the person seriously, not just the chief complaint or the disease.

To this end, we teach our medical students to ask the open-ended question, "Is there anything else you would like to tell me?" at the end of the medical interview. We encourage them then to pause, for quite a while if necessary, to leave the patient enough psychic space to consider their needs and perhaps the real agenda for being there in the first place. This is often not what gets talked about first or second, or even at all if the doctor isn't particularly tuned in or is in a hurry.

At a faculty development session one day, some experts from another institution were describing their training program for the medical interview, which uses video to give the students direct feedback on their patient-interviewing style. At one point, they showed us a series of very short clips of just that last question being asked from a number of different interviews, each student simply asking one patient, "Is there anything else you would like to tell me?" Before showing these clips, we were assigned the task of noticing and later reporting on what was going on.

By the third one, I was doing everything I could to keep from rolling on the floor with laughter. To my surprise, there were a good many blank faces among these highly experienced clinicians, the best of the best, although some caught on quickly. The same thing was happening in clip after clip after clip. But it was so obvious that it was hard to see, just like lots of things that are right under our noses.

In virtually every clip, while the student was saying what they had been taught to say to close the interview, namely, "Is there anything else you would like to tell me?" every single one was noticeably shaking their head from side to side, nonverbally conveying the message, "No, please, don't tell me any more!"

Your Own Authority

When I started work at the medical center, I was given three long white coats that had "Dr. Kabat-Zinn / Department of Medicine" neatly embroidered on the pocket. I was pleased, as a basic scientist with no medical training at all, to be included in the club. In fact, I was honored, deeply moved to be part of such a noble enterprise. Still, those white coats hung on the back of my office door for twenty years, unused.

To me, they were emblematical of exactly what I didn't need in my job as a meditation teacher and MBSR instructor. I suppose they are a good thing for physicians, enhancing as they do the aura of authority and thus perhaps some positive placebo effect with their patients. The aura is augmented further if there is a stethoscope hanging out of the pocket at just the right angle. Young doctors sometimes try in their enthusiasm to go this one better and wear it with studied casualness across the back of the neck and shoulders.

But working in the MBSR clinic, the white coat would have been a true impediment. I have to work overtime as it is to deflect back all the projections I get from people that I am "Mr. Mindfulness" or "Mr. Relaxation," or "Dr. Have-It-All-Together" or "Mr. Wisdom-and-Compassion-Incarnate." The whole point of mindfulness-based stress reduction—and for that matter health promotion in its largest sense—is to challenge and encourage people to become their own authorities, to take more responsibility for their own lives, their own bodies, their own health. I like to emphasize that each person is already the world authority on themselves, or at least could be if they started attending to things more systematically, more mindfully. A great deal of the information each of us needs to learn more about ourselves and our health—information we desperately need in order to grow and to heal and to make effective life choices—is already right at our fingertips, or even more accurately, right beneath our noses.

What is required to participate more fully in our own health and wellbeing—what is now officially called *participatory medicine*—is simply to listen more carefully and trust what we hear and learn by attending to the messages from our own life, from our own body and mind and feelings. This sense of participation and confidence in our own internal resources to be active collaborators in our own health care and our health trajectory across the life span is all too frequently a missing ingredient in medicine. We all have interior resources for healing, for coping more effectively with challenges, for seeing a little more clearly, for being a little more assertive, for asking more questions, for getting by more skillfully. Tapping into those resources is not a replacement for expert medical care, but it is a critically important complement to it if you hope to live a truly healthy life—especially in the face of disease, disability, chronic health conditions, the challenges of aging, and a frequently alienating, intimidating, insensitive, overstressed, and sometimes iatrogenic health-care system.

Developing such a participatory attitude and the engagement that follows from it means taking some degree of responsibility for authoring one's own life and, therefore, assuming some measure of authority over one's own health and well-being. It requires believing in oneself. Deep down, sadly, a lot of us don't.

Mindful inquiry can heal a sense of low self-esteem or the habit of minimizing one's own self-worth or worthiness for the simple reason that a low self-estimation is really a wrong calculation, a misperception of reality. You can see this very clearly when you start to observe your own body or even just your breathing in meditation. You quickly come to see that your body is miraculous on every level, from the atomic and subatomic to the macromolecular, to the cellular, to highly specialized functional tissues, organs, and on and on. It is a veritable galaxy, a marvel, 99.9 percent empty space on one level, and more than half water on another, capable of effortless sentience within the unique constellation that is you, with the most complex arrangement of matter in the known universe right under the vault of your own cranium—the human brain. The body performs amazing feats by the moment with no conscious effort. Our esteem problems stem in large part from our thinking, colored by past experiences, sometimes highly traumatic and damaging in one way or another. We so easily revert to seeing only our shortcomings and blow them out of all proportion. At the same time, we take all our good qualities for granted or fail to acknowledge them at all. Perhaps we get stuck in the often deep and still-bleeding wounds of childhood and forget or never discover that we have golden qualities too. The wounds are important, but so is the larger body and mind space that holds the scars and itself is not scarred. Equally important in this calculus are our inner goodness, our caring, our kindness toward others, the intrinsic wisdom of the body, our capacity to think, to discern, to know what's what. And we do know what's what, much more than we allow. Yet, sadly, instead of seeing in a balanced way, we frequently persist in the habit of projecting onto others that they are okay and we are not.

I balk when people project onto me in this way. I try to reflect those projections back to them as commonsensically as I can, in the hope that they will come to see what they are doing and understand that their appreciation of me is really theirs. The positivity is their own. The gratitude is their own, and if there is a reason for it, that reason resides within them as well, not in me. It is their energy, their beauty, and hopefully, they will come to realize that that is the case—through ongoing practice—and that they need to own it, make use of it, and appreciate its source within themselves. Why should anyone give away their power, especially through projections onto others?

*

[People] measure their esteem of each other by what each has, and not by what each is.... Nothing can bring you peace but yourself.

RALPH WALDO EMERSON, *Self-Reliance*

Wherever You Go, There You Are

Have you ever noticed that there is no running away from anything? That, sooner or later, the things that you don't want to deal with and try to escape from or paper over and pretend aren't there catch up with you—especially if they have to do with old patterns and fears? The romantic notion is that if it's no good over here, you have only to go over there and things will be different. If this job is no good, change jobs. If this partner, wife, spouse is no good, find someone else to love and to love you. If this town is no good, move. If these children are a problem, leave them for other people to look after. The underlying thinking is that the reason for your troubles is outside of you—in the location, in others, in the circumstances. Change the location, change the circumstances, change who you spend time with, and everything will fall into place; you can start over, have a new beginning.

The trouble with this way of seeing is that it conveniently ignores the fact that you carry your head and your heart, and what some would call your "karma," around with you. You cannot escape yourself, try as you might. And what reason, other than pure wishful thinking, would you have to suspect that things would be different or better somewhere else anyway? Sooner or later, the same problems would arise if in fact they stem in large part from your patterns of seeing, thinking, and behaving. Too often, our lives cease working because we cease working at life, because we are unwilling to take responsibility for things as they are in the here and now and work with our difficulties and challenges, our likes and dislikes, rather than becoming prisoners of them. We fail to realize, or we forget, that it is actually possible to taste moments of wellbeing, equanimity, clarity, understanding, and transformation right in the midst of what is here now, however problematic it may be, and to act out of that recognition. But it is easier and less threatening to our sense of self to project the source of our supposed problems onto other people and the environment.

It is so much easier to find fault, to blame, to believe that what is needed is a change on the outside, an escape from the forces that are holding you back, preventing you from growing, from finding happiness. You can even blame yourself for it all and, in the ultimate escape from responsibility, run away—either physically or emotionally or both—feeling that you have made a hopeless mess of things or that you are damaged beyond repair. In either case, you may be succumbing to the toxic belief that you are incapable of true change or growth, and that you need to spare others any more pain by removing yourself from the scene.

The casualties of this way of looking at things are all over the place. Look virtually anywhere, and you will find broken relationships, broken families, broken people—wanderers with no roots, lost, going from this place to that, this job to that, this relationship to that, this idea of salvation to that, in the desperate hope that the right person, the right job, the right place, the right book, the right podcast, the right drug combination will make it all better.

Or feeling isolated, unlovable, and despairing, having given up looking and even making any attempt, however misguided, to find some degree of peace of mind.

By itself, meditation does not confer immunity from this pattern of looking elsewhere for answers and solutions to one's problems. Sometimes people chronically go from one meditation practice to another, from one teacher to another, or from one tradition to another, looking for that special something, that special teaching, that special relationship, that momentary "high" or insight that will open the door to self-understanding and liberation. But such an arc can lead to serious delusion, an unending quest to avoid looking at the actuality of things, what is closest to home and perhaps most painful. Out of fear and a yearning for someone special to see them and to help them to see clearly, people sometimes fall into unhealthy dependency relationships with meditation teachers, forgetting that no matter how good the teacher, ultimately you have to live the inner work yourself, and that work always comes from the cloth of your own life.

Some people even wind up misusing extended teacher-led meditation retreats as a way to keep afloat in their lives rather than as an extended opportunity to look deeply into themselves. On retreat, in a certain way everything is easy. The bare necessities of living are taken care of. The world makes sense. All I have to do is sit and walk, be mindful, stay in the present, be cooked for and fed by a caring staff, listen to the great wisdom that is being put out by people who have worked deeply on themselves and have attained considerable understanding and harmony in their lives, and I will be transformed, inspired to live more fully myself, know how to be in the world, have a better perspective on my own problems.

To a large extent, this is all true. Good teachers and long periods of isolated meditation on retreat can be profoundly valuable and healing, if one is willing to look at everything that comes up during a retreat. But there is also the danger, which needs to be looked out for, that retreats can become a retreat from life in the world, and that one's "transformation" will, in the end, be only skin-deep. Perhaps the glow will last a few days, or weeks, or months after the retreat ends, but then, without careful attending, it might be back to the same old life patterns, thought patterns, and lack of clarity in regard to relationships and life and work in the mainstream world—and thus, looking forward already to the next retreat, or the next great teacher, or a pilgrimage to Asia, or some other romantic fantasy in which things will deepen or become clearer and you will be a better person.

This way of thinking and seeing is an all-too-pervasive trap. There is no successful escaping from yourself in the long run, only transformation. It doesn't matter whether you are using psychedelics or meditation, alcohol or an exotic vacation, divorce or quitting your job. There can be no resolution leading to growth until the present situation has been faced completely and you have opened to it with mindfulness, allowing the roughness of the situation itself to sand down your own rough edges. In other words, you've got to be willing to let life itself become your teacher.

This is the path of working where you find yourself, with what is found here and now. This, then, really is it . . . this place, this relationship, this dilemma, this job, this pandemic, this moment. The challenge of mindfulness is to work with the very circumstances that you find yourself in—no matter how unpleasant, how discouraging, how limited, how unending and stuck they may appear to be—and to make sure that you have done everything in your power to use their energies to transform yourself before you decide to cut your losses and move on—which at times is certainly the only right decision. But it is right here, with things exactly as they are, unadorned, that the real work of mindfulness and heartfulness unfolds.

So, if you think your meditation practice is dull, or no good, or that the conditions aren't right where you find yourself, and you think that if only you were in a cave in the Himalayas, or at an Asian monastery, or on a beach in the tropics, or at a retreat in some natural setting, things would be better, your meditation stronger...think again. When you go to your cave or your beach or your retreat, there you would be, with the same mind, the same body, the very same breath that you already have here. After fifteen minutes or so in the cave, you might get lonely, or want more light, or the roof might drip water on you. If you were on the beach, it might be raining or cold. If you were on retreat, you might not like the teachers, or the food, or your room. There is always something to dislike. So why not let go and admit that you might as well be at home all the time, in every moment, wherever you are? Right in that moment, which when it arises, is always *this* moment, you touch the core of your being and invite mindfulness to enter and heal. If you understand this, then and only then will the cave, the monastery, the beach, the retreat center offer up their true richness to you. But so will all other moments and places.

My foot slips on a narrow ledge: in that split second, as needles of fear pierce heart and temples, eternity intersects with present time. Thought and action are not different, and stone, air, ice, sun, fear, and self are one. What is exhilarating is to extend this acute awareness into ordinary moments, in the moment-by-moment experiencing of the lammergeier and the wolf, which, finding themselves at the center of things, have no need for any secret of true being. In this very breath that we take now lies the secret that all great teachers try to tell us, what one lama refers to as "the precision and openness and intelligence of the present." The purpose of meditation practice is not enlightenment; it is to pay attention even at unextraordinary times, to be of the present, nothing-but-the-present, to bear this mindfulness of now into each event of ordinary life.

PETER MATTHIESSEN, *The Snow Leopard*

Going Upstairs

Occasions to practice mindfulness in everyday life abound. Going upstairs is a good one for me. I do it hundreds of times a day when I'm at home. Usually I need something from upstairs or to speak with someone upstairs, but my long-term agenda is to be down-stairs, so I'm frequently torn between two places. I'm on my way up only to be on my way down after I've found what I'm looking for, or gone to the bathroom, or whatever.

So I discover that I am frequently pulled by my need to be somewhere else, or by the next thing I think needs to hap-pen, or the next place I think I'm supposed to be. When I find myself racing upstairs, usually two steps at a time, I sometimes have the presence of mind to catch myself in mid–frenetic dash. I become conscious of being slightly out of breath, aware that my heart is racing as well as my mind, that the whole of my being in that moment is being driven by some hurried purpose that often even eludes me by the time I'm up there.

When I am able to capture in awareness this rising wave of energy while still at the bottom of the stairs or starting on my way up, I will sometimes slow my ascent—not just one step at a time, but really slow, maybe one breath cycle per step, reminding myself that there is really no place I have to go and nothing I have to get that can't wait another moment for the sake of being fully in this one.

I find that when I remember to do this, I am more in touch along the way and more centered at the top. I also find that there is hardly ever an outward hurry. Only an inner one, usually driven by impatience and a mindless type of anxious thinking, which varies from so subtle I have to listen carefully to detect it at all, to so dominant that almost nothing will deflect its momentum. But even then, I can be aware of it and of its consequences, and this awareness by itself helps keep me from losing myself entirely in the turbulence of the mind in those moments. And, as you might guess, this works going down the stairs too, but here, because the pull of gravity is working for me, it's even more of a challenge to slow things down.

TRY: Using ordinary, repetitive occasions in your own home— the number of floors is of no consequence—as invitations to practice mindfulness. Going to the front door, sitting down at your laptop, looking for your phone, seeking out someone else in the house to speak with, going to the bathroom, getting the laundry out of the dryer, putting it away, going to the refrigerator can all be occasions to slow down and be more in touch with each present moment. Notice the sensations that drive you toward the phone or the doorbell on the first ring or the Pavlovian response to notifications, if your notifications are even on. Why does your response time have to be so fast that it pulls you out of the life you were living in the preceding moment? Can these transitions become more graceful? Can you be more where you find yourself all the time, in every moment? And without striving or forcing anything, a true non-doing?

You might also play with being present for everyday habitual occurrences, things like taking a shower or eating. When you are in the shower, are you really in the shower? Do you feel the water on your skin, or are you someplace else, lost in thought, missing the shower altogether? Eating is another good occasion for mindfulness practice. Are you tasting your food? Are you aware of how fast, how much, when, where, and what you are eating? Can you turn your entire day as it unfolds into an occasion to be present or to bring yourself back to the present moment, over and over again, with the lightest of touches, and, at the same time, as if your life depended on it?

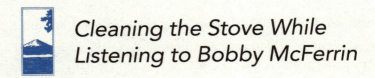

Cleaning the Stove While Listening to Bobby McFerrin

I can lose myself and find myself simultaneously while cleaning the kitchen stove. This is a great, if rare, occasion for mindfulness practice. Because I don't do it regularly, it is quite a challenge by the time I get around to it, and there are lots of levels of clean to aim for. I play—within reason—with getting the stove to look as if it were brand new by the time I'm finished.

I use a scrubber that is abrasive enough to get the caked food off if I rub hard enough with baking soda, but not so abrasive that I scratch the finish. I take off the burner elements and the pans underneath, even the knobs, and soak them in the sink, to be tackled at the end. Then I scrub every square inch of stove surface, favoring a circular motion at times, at others a back-and-forth. It all depends on the location and topology of the crud. I get into the round and round or the back-and-forth, feeling the motion in my whole body, no longer trying to clean the stove so it will look nice, only moving, moving, watching, watching as things change slowly before my eyes. At the end, I wipe the surfaces carefully with a damp sponge.

Music adds to the experience at times. Other times, I prefer silence for my work. One Saturday morning, long ago, a tape by Bobby McFerrin (the fact that it was a tape tells you how long ago it was) was playing in the cassette player when the occasion arose to clean the stove. So cleaning became dancing, McFerrin's playful incantations, sounds, and rhythms blending together and merging with the movements of my body, sounds unfolding in motion, sensations in my arm aplenty, modulations in finger pressure on the scrubber as required, caked remains of former cookings slowly changing form and disappearing, all rising and falling in awareness with the perfect pitch and magical incantations of his voice—pure music to the ears. One big dance of presence, a celebration of now. And, at the end, a clean stove. The voice inside that ordinarily claims credit for such things ("See how clean I got the stove?") and seeks approval for it ("Didn't I do a good job?") stirs, but is quickly held in a larger understanding and appreciation of what has transpired.

Mindfully speaking, I can't get away with claiming that "I" cleaned the stove. It's more like the stove cleaned itself, with the help of Bobby McFerrin, the scrubber, the baking soda, and the sponge, with guest appearances by hot water, muscle, and a string of present moments.

What Is My Job on the Planet with a Capital J?

"What is my job on the planet?" is one question we might do well to ask ourselves over and over again—especially when we are in the third, fourth, and fifth decades of life—but the earlier the better in any event. Otherwise, we may wind up doing somebody else's job and not even know it. And what's more, that somebody else might be a figment of our own imagination and maybe a prisoner of it as well. The question could be thought of as a Zen koan—and treated with the respect it deserves. It is not a matter of privilege, although at first blush it might seem that way. Rather, it calls out a deep and intuitive inquiry into one's karmic trajectory and one's heart's unique passions, longings, and gifts—and how they change and evolve over time.

As thinking creatures, packaged, as are all life-forms, in unique organismic units we call bodies, and simultaneously totally and impersonally embedded in the warp and woof of life's ceaseless unfolding, we have a singular capacity to take responsibility for our unique piece of what it means to be alive, at least while we have our brief moment in the sun. But we also have the singular capacity of letting our thinking mind entirely cloud our transit through this world. We are at risk of never realizing our radical uniqueness—at least as long as we remain in the shadow cast by our thought habits and conditioning.

Buckminster Fuller, the discoverer/inventor of the geodesic dome, at age thirty-two contemplated suicide for a few hours one night at the edge of Lake Michigan, as the story goes, after a series of business failures that left him feeling he had made such a mess of his life that the best move would be for him to remove himself from the scene and make things simpler for his wife and infant daughter. Apparently everything he had touched or undertaken had turned to dust in spite of his incredible creativity and imagination, which were only recognized later. However, instead of ending his life, Fuller decided (perhaps because of his deep conviction of the underlying unity and order of the universe, of which he knew himself to be an integral part) to live from then on as if he had died that night.

Being dead, he wouldn't have to worry about how things worked out any longer for himself personally and would be free to devote himself to living as a representative of the universe. The rest of his life would be a gift. Instead of living for himself, he would devote himself to asking, "What is it on this planet [which he referred to as Spaceship Earth] that needs doing that I know something about, that probably won't happen unless I take responsibility for it?" He decided he would just ask that question continuously and do what came to him, following his nose. In this way, working for humanity as an employee of the universe at large, you get to modify and contribute to your locale by who you are, how you are, and what you do. But it's no longer personal. It's just part of the totality of the universe expressing itself. And somehow, often quite mysteriously, the wherewithal to survive and even thrive somehow emerges. The universe collaborates.

Rarely do we question and then contemplate with determination what our hearts are calling us to do and to be. I like to frame such efforts in question form: "What is my job on the planet with a capital J?" or "What do I care about so much that I would pay to do it?" If I ask such a question and I don't come up with an answer, other than "I don't know," then I just keep asking the question. If you start reflecting on such questions when you're in your twenties, by the time you are thirty-five or forty, or fifty or sixty, the inquiry itself may have led you a few places that you would not have gone had you merely followed mainstream conventions, or your parents' expectations for you, or even worse, your own usually unexamined self-limiting beliefs and assumptions. And often, the inquiry is not only healthy for yourself; it is healthy for the larger world for you to ask such questions of yourself and trust in your own longing, in your interests, in your intuition of what is yours to do and what is not yours to do, and disregard the naysayers—the ones in the world and the ones in your head.

You can start asking this question anytime, at any age. There is never a time of life when it would not have a profound effect on your view of things and the choices you make. It may not mean that you will change what you do, but it may mean that you will want to change how you see it or hold it, and perhaps how you do it. Once the universe is your employer, very interesting things start to happen, even if someone else is cutting your paycheck. But you do have to be patient. It takes time to grow this way of being in your life. The place to start of course is right here. The best time? How about now?

You never know what will come of such introspections. Fuller himself was fond of stating that what seems to be happening at the moment is never the full story of what is really going on. He liked to point out that for the honeybee, it is the honey that is important. But the bee is at the same time nature's vehicle for carrying out cross-pollination of the flowers and crops—a treasure we could be on the verge of losing as bee colonies die off from various environmental pressures, including new invasive parasites. Interconnectedness is a fundamental principle of nature. Nothing is isolated. Each event connects with others. Things are constantly unfolding on different levels. It's for us to perceive the warp and woof of it all as best we can and learn to follow our own threads through the tapestry of life with authenticity and resolve—and not be intimidated by barriers of any kind: racial, social, economic, gender-based, institutional, or personal.

Fuller believed in an underlying architecture of nature, in which form and function are inextricably linked. He believed that nature's blueprints would make sense and would have practical relevance to our lives on many levels. Before he died, X-ray crystallographic studies had demonstrated that many viruses—submicroscopic assemblies of macromolecules on the edge of life itself—that we are now all too familiar with, courtesy of COVID—are structured along the same geodesic principles as those he discovered by playing around with polyhedra.

Fuller didn't live long enough to see it, but in addition to all his other seminal inventions and ideas, a whole new field of chemistry opened up around the unpredicted discovery of soccer-ball-like carbon compounds with remarkable properties that quickly became known as Buckminsterfullerenes, or buckyballs. While playing in his sandbox, following his own path, his musings led to discoveries and worlds he never dreamed of. So can yours. Fuller never thought of himself as special in any sense, just a regular person who liked to play with ideas and with forms. His motto was, "If I can understand it, anybody can understand it."

*

Insist on yourself; never imitate. Your own gift you can present every moment with the cumulative force of a whole life's cultivation; but of the adopted talent of another you have only an extemporaneous half possession. . . . Do that which is assigned to you, and you cannot hope too much or dare too much.

RALPH WALDO EMERSON, *Self-Reliance*

Mount Analogue

He may. But in the end, it's the mountain that will decide who will climb it.

EVEREST CLIMB LEADER when asked one
year whether an older veteran climber on the
team would get a chance at the summit

There are outer mountains and inner mountains. In either case, their very presence beckons to us, calls us to ascend. Perhaps the full teaching of a mountain is that you carry the whole mountain inside yourself, the outer one as well as the inner one. And sometimes you search and search for the mountain without finding it until the time comes when you are sufficiently motivated and prepared to find a way through, first to the base, then to the summit. The mountain climb is a powerful metaphor for the life quest, the spiritual journey, the path of growth, transformation, and understanding. The arduous difficulties we encounter along the way embody the very challenges we need in order to stretch ourselves and thereby expand our boundaries. In the end, it is life itself that is the mountain, the teacher, serving us up perfect opportunities to do the inner work of growing in strength and wisdom and in understanding and compassion for others and for the world itself. And we sure have a lot of learning and growing to do once we choose to make the journey. The risks are considerable, the sacrifices awesome, the outcome always uncertain. Ultimately, it is the climb itself that is the adventure, not just standing at the top.

First we learn what it's like at the base. Only later do we encounter the slopes, and finally, perhaps, the top. But you can't stay at the top of a mountain. The journey up is not complete without the descent, the stepping back and seeing the whole again from afar. Having been at the summit, however, you have gained a new perspective, and it may change your way of seeing forever.

In a wonderfully unfinished story called "Mount Analogue," René Daumal once mapped a piece of this inward adventure. The part I remember most vividly involves the rule on Mount Analogue that before you move up the mountain to your next encampment, you must replenish the camp you are leaving for those who will come after you, and go down the mountain a ways to share with the other climbers your knowledge from farther up so that they may have some benefit from what you have learned so far on your own ascent.

In a way, that's all any of us do when we teach. As best we can, we show others what we have seen up to now. It's at best a progress report, a map of our experiences, by no means the absolute truth. And so the adventure unfolds. We are all on Mount Analogue together. And we need each other's help.

Interconnectedness and Impermanence

It seems we know full well from childhood that everything is connected to everything else in certain ways, that this happens because that happened, that for this to happen, that has to happen. Just recall all those old folktales, such as the one about the fox who drinks most of an old woman's pail of milk that she neglected to watch as she was gathering wood for a fire. She cuts off his tail in a fit of anger. The fox asks for his tail back, and the old woman says she will sew his tail back on for him if he will give her back her milk. So he goes to the cow in the field and asks for some milk, and the cow says she will give the fox some milk if the fox brings her some grass. So the fox goes to the field and asks for some grass, and the field says, "Bring me some water." So he goes to the stream and asks for water and the stream says, "Bring me a jug." This goes on until a miller, out of kindness and sympathy, gives the fox some grain to give the hen to get the egg to give to the peddler to get the bead to give to the maiden to get the jug to fetch the water . . . and so the fox gets his tail sewn back on and goes away happy. The lesson: This has to happen in order for that to happen. Nothing comes from nothing. Everything has antecedents. Even the miller's kindness came from somewhere.

Looking deeply into any process, we can see that the same applies. No sunlight, no life. No water, no life. No plants, no

219

chlorophyll; no chlorophyll, no photosynthesis; no photosynthesis, no oxygen for animals to breathe. No parents, no you. No trucks, no food in the cities. No truck manufacturers, no trucks. No steelworkers, no steel for the manufacturers. No mining, no steel for the steelworkers. No food, no steelworkers. No rain, no food. No sunlight, no rain. No conditions for star and planet formation in the formative universe, no Sun and no Earth. These relationships are not always simple and linear. Usually, things are embedded in a complex web of finely balanced interconnections. Certainly what we call life, or health, or the biosphere, are all complex systems of interconnections, with no absolute starting point or end point.

So we see the futility and the danger of letting our thinking make any object or circumstance into an absolutely separate existence without being mindful of interconnectedness and flux. Everything is related to everything else and, in a way, simultaneously contains everything else and is contained by everything else. What is more, everything is in flux. Stars are born, go through stages, and die. Planets also have a rhythm of formation and ultimate demise. New cars are already on their way to the junk heap before they leave the factory. This awareness might truly enhance our appreciation of what we might call the law of impermanence, and help us to take things and circumstances and relationships less for granted while they are around. We might appreciate life more, people more, food more, opinions more, moments more, if we perceive, by our own looking more deeply into them, that everything we are in contact with connects us to the whole world in each moment, and that things and other people, and even places and circumstances, are only here temporarily, that everything arises and ultimately passes away. It makes now so much more interesting. In fact, it makes now everything.

Mindfulness of breathing is one string on which the beads of our experience, our thoughts, our feelings, our emotions, our perceptions, our impulses, our understanding, our very consciousness can be threaded. The necklace created is something new—not a thing really but a new way of seeing, a new way of being, a new way of experiencing that permits a new way of acting in the world. This new way seems to connect what seems to be isolated. But, actually, nothing is ever isolated. It's our way of seeing that creates and maintains separation.

This new way of seeing and new way of being holds life fragments and accords them proper place. It honors each moment in its own fullness within a larger fullness. Mindfulness practice is simply the ongoing discovery of the thread of interconnectedness. At some point, we may even come to see that it is not quite correct to say that we are doing the threading. It's more like we become conscious of a connectedness, an interrelationality, a fluxing that has been here all the time. We have climbed to a vantage point from which we can more readily perceive wholeness and can cradle the flow of present moments in awareness. The flow of the breath and the flow of present moments interpenetrate, beads and thread together giving something larger.

*

One merges into another, groups melt into ecological groups until the time when what we know as life meets and enters what we think of as non-life: barnacle and rock, rock and earth, earth and tree, tree and rain and air.... And it is a strange thing that most of the feeling we call religious, most of the mystical outcrying which is one of the most prized and used and desired reactions of our species, is really the understanding and the attempt to say that man [in the old way of speaking: i.e., a human being] is related to the whole thing, related inextricably to all reality, known and unknowable. This is a simple thing to say, but the profound feeling of it made a Jesus, a St. Augustine, a St. Francis, a Roger Bacon, a Charles Darwin, and an Einstein. Each of them in his own tempo and with his own voice discovered and reaffirmed with astonishment the knowledge that all things are one thing and that one thing is all things—plankton, a shimmering phosphorescence on the sea and spinning planets and the expanding universe, all bound together by the elastic string of time.

JOHN STEINBECK AND EDWARD F. RICKETTS,
Sea of Cortez

Non-Harming—Ahimsa

A friend came back after several years in Nepal and India in 1973 and said of himself, "If I can't do anything useful, at least I would like to do as little harm as possible."

I guess you can bring back all sorts of communicable things from distant parts if you're not careful. I was infected with the idea of ahimsa right then and there in my Cambridge living room, and I have never forgotten the moment it happened. I had heard it before. The attitude of non-harming lies at the heart of yoga practice and of the Hippocratic Oath. It was the underlying principle of Gandhi's revolution and of his personal meditation practice. But there was something about the sincerity with which my friend Paul made his comment, coupled with the incongruity of the person I thought I knew saying it, that impressed me. It struck me as a good way to relate to the world and to oneself. Why not try to live so as to cause as little damage and suffering as possible? If we lived that way, we wouldn't have the insane levels of violence that dominate our lives and our thinking today. And we would be more generous toward ourselves as well, on the meditation cushion and off it.

Like any other view, non-harming may be a terrific principle, but it's the living of it that counts. You can start practicing ahimsa's gentleness on yourself and in your life with others in any moment.

Do you sometimes find that you are hard on yourself and put yourself down? Remember ahimsa in that moment. See what you are doing, and let it go.

Do you talk about others behind their backs? Ahimsa.

Do you push yourself beyond your limits with no regard for your body and your wellbeing? Ahimsa.

Do you cause other people pain or grief? Ahimsa. It is easy to relate with ahimsa to someone who doesn't threaten you. The test is in how you will relate to a person or situation when you do feel threatened.

The willingness to harm or hurt comes ultimately out of fear. Non-harming requires that you see your own fears and that you understand them and own them. Owning them means taking responsibility for them. Taking responsibility means not letting fear completely dictate your view or your actions. Only mindfulness of our own clinging and rejecting, and a willingness to grapple with these constricted mind states, however painful the encounter, can free us from this sad circle of suffering. Without a daily embodiment through intentional cultivation in formal and informal practice, lofty ideals tend to succumb in the end to ill-conceived and small-minded self-interest.

*

Ahimsa is the attribute of the soul, and therefore, to be practiced by everybody in all the affairs of life. If it cannot be practiced in all departments, it has no practical value.

MAHATMA GANDHI

*

If you can't love King George V, say, or Sir Winston Churchill, start with your wife, or your husband, or your children. Try to put their welfare first and your own last every minute of the day, and let the circle of your love expand from there. As long as you are trying your very best, there can be no question of failure.

MAHATMA GANDHI

Karma

Seung Sahn, my Korean Zen teacher, was fond of saying that daily meditation practice could turn bad karma into good karma. I always chalked this up to a quaint moralistic sales pitch. It took me years to get the point. I guess that's my karma.

Karma means that this happens because that happened. B is connected in some way to A, every effect has an antecedent cause, and every cause an effect that is its measure and its consequence, at least at the non-quantum level. Overall, when we speak of a person's karma, it means the sum total of the person's direction in life and the tenor of the things that occur around that person, caused by antecedent conditions, actions, thoughts, feelings, sense impressions, desires. Karma is often wrongly confused with the notion of a fixed destiny. It is more like an accumulation of tendencies that can lock us into particular behavior patterns, which themselves result in further accumulations of tendencies of a similar nature. So, it is easy to become imprisoned by our karma and to think that the cause always lies elsewhere—with other people and conditions beyond our control, never within ourselves. But it is not fated to be a prisoner of old karma. It is always possible to change your karma. You can make new karma. But there is only one time that you ever have to do it in. Can you guess when that might be?

Here's how mindfulness changes karma. When you sit, you are not allowing your impulses to translate into action. For the time being, at least, you are just watching them if and when they arise. Looking at them, you quickly see that all impulses in the mind arise and pass away, that they have a life of their own, that they are not you but just thinking, and that you do not have to be ruled by them. Not feeding or reacting to impulses, you come to apprehend directly their nature as thoughts. With ongoing regular practice, you can actually see that this process burns up destructive impulses in the fires of increasing concentration, non-doing, clear seeing, and equanimity. At the same time, creative insights and creative impulses are no longer squeezed out so much by the more turbulent, destructive ones. They are nourished as they are perceived and held in awareness. Mindfulness can thereby refashion the links in the chain of actions and consequences, and in doing so it unchains us, frees us, and opens up new directions and choices for us through the moments we call life, in spite of our conditioning and the causes and conditions that generate suffering—including injustices of all kinds. Without some grounding in mindfulness as a reliable way of being in wise relationship to experiences, whatever they might be—inner or outer, pleasant, unpleasant, or neither—we can all too easily get caught up and stuck in the feeling tone (whether we find an experience momentarily pleasant, unpleasant, or neither) and momentum coming out of a past moment, with no clue to our own imprisonment and, thus, no way out. In that moment, our dilemma always seems to be the other person's fault, or the world's fault, so our own highly conditioned views and feelings and actions are always seen as justified. The present moment is never a new beginning only because we keep it from becoming one.

How else to explain, for example, the all-too-common observation that two people who have lived their whole adult lives together, had children together, tasted success in their own realms to a degree not usually achieved, might in their later years, when by all accounts they should be enjoying the fruits of their labors, each blame the other for making life miserable, for feeling isolated, trapped in a bad dream, so mistreated and abused that anger and hurt are the fabric of each day? Karma. In one form or another, you see it over and over again in relationships gone sour or missing something fundamental from the start, the absence of which invites sadness, bitterness, hurt. Sooner or later, we are most likely to reap that which we have sown. Practice anger and isolation in a relationship for forty years, and you wind up imprisoned in anger and isolation. No big surprise. And it is hardly satisfactory to apportion blame at that point, or ever, actually.

Ultimately, it is our mindlessness that imprisons us. We get better and better at being out of touch with the full range of our possibilities and more and more stuck in our cultivated-over-a-lifetime habits of not-seeing but only reacting and blaming.

Working in prisons, I got to see the results of so-called bad karma up close, although it's hardly any different outside the prison walls. Every inmate has a story of one thing leading to another. After all, that's what stories are. One thing leading to another. Many hardly know what happened to them, what went wrong. Usually it's a long chain of events starting with parents and family, the culture of the streets, poverty and violence, trusting people you shouldn't, looking for an easy buck, soothing the hurt and dulling the senses with alcohol and other chemicals that cloud mind and body. Drugs do it, but so do histories of legalized injustice, violence, deprivation, and thwarted aspirations. They tend to warp thoughts and feelings, actions and values, leaving few avenues for modulating or even recognizing hurtful, cruel, destructive, and self-destructive impulses or cravings.

And so, in one moment, which all your other moments led up to, unbeknownst to you, you can "lose your mind," commit an irreversible act, and then experience the myriad ways it shapes future moments. Everything has consequences, whether we know it or not, whether we are "apprehended" by the police or not. We are always caught. Caught in the karma of it. We build our own prisons every day. In one way, my friends in prison made their choices, whether they knew it or not. In other ways, they didn't have choices. Or if there were choices, they never knew they were there or how to make them. In a certain sense, we are all imprisoned—imprisoned by our own unawareness and its often severe consequences.

So, once again, we encounter what Buddhists call "unawareness," or ignorance. It is ignorance of how unexamined impulses, especially those colored by greed or hatred, however justified, rationalized, or technically legal, can warp one's mind and one's life. Such mind states affect us all, sometimes in big dramatic ways but most often by more subtle paths. We can all be imprisoned by incessant wanting, by a mind clouded with ideas and opinions it clings to as if they were truths.

If we hope to change our karma, we have to stop making those things happen that cloud mind and body and color our every action. It doesn't mean doing good deeds. It means knowing who you are and that you are not your karma, whatever it may be at this moment. It means aligning yourself with the way things actually are and what is truly called for in this moment outside of your own severe and often opaque-to-you conditioning. It means seeing clearly. That is an entirely different form of "apprehension"—the apprehending of things as they are.

Where to start? Why not with your own mind? After all, it is the instrument through which all your thoughts and emotions, impulses and perceptions, beliefs and assumptions are translated into actions in the world. When you stop outward activity for some time and practice being still, right here, in this moment, with, say, a decision and accompanying resolve to sit in formal meditation practice for a period of clock time—and you stay there (which in that moment would be experienced as *here*) no matter what—you are already breaking the flow of old karma and creating entirely new and healthier karma in your opening to and residing in non-doing and not-knowing. Herein lies the root of changing one's own life direction, a potential turning point in a life fully lived. How?

Because the very act of stopping, of nurturing moments of non-doing, of simply watching, attending, and letting settle the angry or impulsive or agitated mind from lack of feeding, puts you on an entirely different footing vis-à-vis the future. It is only by being fully in this moment that any future moment might be one of greater understanding, clarity, and kindness, one less dominated by fear or hurt, anger or resentment, and more by dignity and a wise acceptance of things as they are. Only what happens now happens later. If there is no mindfulness or equanimity or compassion now, in the only time we ever have to invite them in and nourish ourselves with their energies, how likely is it that it will magically appear later, under stress or duress?

*

The idea that the soul will join with the ecstatic
just because the body is rotten—
that is all fantasy.
What is found now is found then.

KABIR

Wholeness and Oneness

When we are in touch with being whole, we feel at one with everything—intimately, intrinsically, and inextricably connected with the entire universe. When we feel at one with everything, we feel whole ourselves, complete as we are right in this very moment.

Sitting still or lying still, in *any* moment, we can reconnect with our body, transcend the body, merge with the breath, with the air and the sky, with the planet, with the entirety of things. We experience ourselves as whole and simultaneously folded into larger and larger wholes. Even a taste or a glimpse of interconnectedness brings a direct experience of belonging, a sense of being an intimate part of things, of being at home wherever we are. We may taste and wonder at an ancient timelessness beyond individual birth and death, and simultaneously experience the fleeting brevity of this life as we pass through it, the impermanence of our ties to our ever-changing body, to this moment, to each other.

Experiencing our wholeness and our oneness, and their interconnectedness, directly in the meditation practice, we may find ourselves recognizing and coming to terms with things as they are, which as we have seen, does not imply passive resignation by any stretch of the imagination when it comes to changing what needs changing, to whatever degree we can contribute to that calling. A gradual deepening of understanding and compassion may emerge over time, along with, perhaps, a commitment to heal and transform the roots of unnecessary suffering in the world in ways both little and big, depending on your own karmic inclinations and the scope of what you most love and honor.

Wholeness is the root of everything that the words "health," "healing," and "holy" signify in our language and our culture. When we perceive our intrinsic wholeness, there is truly no place to go and nothing to do. Thus, we are free to choose a path for ourselves. Wholeness becomes available in engagements of both doing and non-doing. We discover that stillness is here, within ourselves, at all times. And as we give ourselves over to stillness, touch it, taste it, listen to it, the body cannot but touch it, taste it, listen to it as well, and in so doing, let go completely into it. The mind too comes to listen and, in the hearing itself, knows at least a moment of stillness and of peace. Open and receptive, we find balance and harmony right here, infinite space folded into this place, infinite time folded into this moment.

*

Ordinary men hate solitude.

But the Master makes use of it,

embracing his aloneness, realizing

he is one with the whole universe

LAO-TZU, *Tao-te-Ching*

*

Peace comes within the souls of men

When they realize their oneness with the universe.

BLACK ELK

*

Siddhartha listened. He was now listening intently, completely absorbed, quite empty, taking in everything. He felt
that he had now completely learned the art of listening. He
had often heard all this before, all these numerous voices in
the river, but today they sounded different. He could no longer distinguish the different voices—the merry voice from
the weeping voice, the childish voice from the manly voice.
They all belonged to each other: the lament of those who
yearn, the laughter of the wise, the cry of indignation and
the groan of the dying. They were all interwoven and inter-
locked, entwined in a thousand ways. And all the voices, all
the goals, all the pleasures, all the good and evil, all of them
together was the world. All of them together was the stream

of events, the music of life. When Siddhartha listened attentively to this river, to this song of a thousand voices, when he did not listen to the sorrow or the laughter, when he did not bind his soul to any one particular voice and absorb it in his Self, but heard them all, the whole, the unity, then the great song of a thousand voices consisted of one word.

HERMANN HESSE, *Siddhartha*

*

What is needed is to learn afresh, to observe, and to discover for ourselves, the meaning of wholeness.

DAVID BOHM, *Wholeness and the Implicate Order*

*

I am large; I contain multitudes.

WALT WHITMAN, *Leaves of Grass*

Eachness and Suchness

Wholeness experienced firsthand cannot be tyrannical, for it is infinite in its diversity and finds itself mirrored and embedded in each particular, like the Hindu god Indra's net, a symbol of the interconnected universe, which has jewels at all the vertices, each facet of each diamond capturing the reflections of the entire net and so containing the whole. Some would have us worship uniformly at the altar of oneness, using the *idea* of unity rather than an ongoing encounter with it to, steamroller-like, flatten out all differences. That is the function of propaganda, the willful promotion of lies and half-truths, veritably the way of dominance, duplicity, subjugation, and death. The antidote lies in recognizing the unique qualities of this *and* that, their particular individuality, properties, and virtues—in other words, in their eachness and their suchness. Here is where all poetry and art, science and life, wonder and awe, ethics and equity, grace and abundance reside.

All faces resemble each other, yet how easily we see in each uniqueness, individuality, an identity. How deeply we value these differences. The ocean is one inseparable whole, but it has countless waves, every one different from all the others; it has currents, each unique, ever changing; the bottom is a landscape all its own, different everywhere; similarly the shoreline. The atmosphere is whole, but its currents have unique signatures, even though they are just wind. Life on earth is a whole, yet it expresses itself in unique time-bound bodies, microscopic or visible, plant or animal, extinct or living. So there can be no privileged one *place* to be. There can be no one *way* to be, no one way to practice, no one way to learn, no one way to love, no one way to grow or to heal, no one way to live, no one way to feel, no one thing to know or be known. The particulars count. And that means you. You count too.

*

The Chicadee
The chicadee
Hops near to me.

THOREAU

*

The man pulling radishes
pointed the way
with a radish.

ISSA

*

Old pond,
frog jumps in—
splash.

BASHO

*

Midnight. No waves,
no wind, the empty boat
is flooded with moonlight.

DOGEN

Get the idea?

What Is This?

The spirit of inquiry is fundamental to living mindfully. Inquiry is not just a way to solve problems. It is a way to make sure you are staying in touch with the basic mystery of life itself and of our presence here. Who am I? Where am I going? What does it mean to be? What does it mean to be a . . . and you fill in the blank: man, woman, nonbinary person, trans person; child, parent, student, worker, boss, inmate, person without a secure place to live?

And to keep the questioning going: What is my karma? Where am I now? What is my way? What is my job on the planet with a capital *J*?

Inquiry doesn't mean looking for answers, especially quick answers that come out of superficial thinking. It means asking without expecting answers, just pondering the question, carrying the wondering with you, letting it marinate, percolate, bubble, cook, ripen, come in and out of awareness, just as everything else comes in and out of awareness. It means deep listening. To yourself, to others, to the world.

You don't have to be still to inquire. Inquiry and mindfulness can occur simultaneously in the unfolding of your daily life. In fact, inquiry and mindfulness are one and the same thing, come to from different directions. You can ponder "What am I" or "What is this?" or "Where am I going?" or "What is my job?" as you are fixing a car, walking to work, doing the dishes, listening to your daughter sing on a starlit spring evening, or looking for a job online.

Problems of all shapes and sizes come up all the time in life. They range from the trivial to the profound to the overwhelming. The challenge here is to meet them with inquiry, in the spirit of mindfulness. It would mean asking, "What is this thought, this feeling, this dilemma?" "How am I going to deal with it?" Or even, "Am I willing to deal with it or even acknowledge it?"

The first step is to acknowledge that there is a problem, which means there is strain or tension or disharmony of some kind. It might take us forty or fifty years to even come close to acknowledging some of the big demons we carry. But maybe that's okay too. There's no timetable for inquiry. It's like a pot sitting on your shelf. It's ready to do the cooking whenever you are ready to take it down, put something in it, and heat it on the stove. But it is a very good thing from the perspective of growing into yourself when "whenever" collapses into now.

Inquiry means asking questions, over and over again. Do we have the courage to look at something, whatever it is, and to inquire, What is this? What is going on? It involves looking deeply for a sustained period, questioning, questioning, What is this? What is wrong? What is at the root of the problem? What is the evidence? What are the connections? What would a happy solution look like? Questioning, questioning, continually questioning. Listening, listening, listening—to yourself, to others, to the world.

Inquiry is not so much thinking about answers, although the questioning will produce a lot of thoughts that look like answers. It really involves just listening to the thinking that your questioning evokes, as if you were sitting by the stream of your own thoughts, listening to the water flow over and around the rocks, listening, listening, and watching the occasional leaf, or twig, or bubble as it is carried along.

Selfing

The true value of a human being is determined primarily by the measure and sense in which he has attained liberation from the self.

ALBERT EINSTEIN, *The World as I See It*

"I," "me," and "mine" are products of our thinking. My old friend and Dharma brother, Larry Rosenberg, founder of the Cambridge Insight Meditation Center, refers to it as "selfing," that inevitable and incorrigible tendency to construct out of almost everything and every situation an "I," a "me," and a "mine" and then to operate in the world from that limited perspective that is mostly fantasy and defense. Hardly a moment passes that this doesn't happen. But it is so much a part of the fabric of our world that it goes completely unnoticed, much as the proverbial fish has no knowledge of water, so thoroughly is it immersed in it. You can see this for yourself easily enough whether you are meditating in silence or just living a five-minute segment of your life. Out of virtually any and every moment and experience, our thinking mind constructs "my" moment, "my" experience, "my" child, "my" hunger, "my" desire, "my" opinion, "my" way, "my" authority, "my" future, "my" knowledge, "my" body, "my" mind, "my" house, "my" land, "my" idea, "my" feelings, "my" car, "my" problem.

If you observe this process of selfing with sustained attention and inquiry, you will see that what we call "the self" is really a construct, a fabrication of our own mind, and hardly a permanent one, either. If you search deeply for a stable, indivisible self, for the core "you" that underlies "your" experience, you are not likely to find it other than in more thinking. You might say you are your name, but that is not quite accurate. Your name is just a label. The same is true of your age, your gender, your opinions, and so on. None are fundamental to who you are.

When you inquire in this way as deeply as you can follow the thread into who you are or what you are, you are almost sure to find that there is no solid place to land. If you ask, "Who is the I who is asking who am I?" ultimately you come to "I don't know." The "I" just appears as a construct that is known by its attributes, none of which, taken singly or together, really makes up the whole of who you are. Moreover, the "I" construct has the tendency continually to dissolve and reconstruct itself, virtually moment by moment. It also has a strong tendency to feel diminished, small, insecure, and uncertain, since its existence is so tenuous to begin with. This makes the tyranny and suffering associated with unawareness of how much we are caught up in the personal pronouns "I," "me," and "mine" only that much worse.

Then there is the problem of outside forces. The "I" tends to feel good when outside circumstances are supporting its belief in its own goodness and bad when it runs into criticism, difficulties, and what it perceives as obstacles and defeats. Here perhaps lies a major explanation for depression and diminished self-esteem in so many of us. We aren't really aware of this constructed aspect of our identity process. This makes it easy for us to lose our balance and fall into the thought stream, to feel vulnerable and inconsequential when we are not propped up and reinforced in our need for approval or for feeling important. We are likely to continually seek interior stability through outside rewards, through material possessions and status, and from others who love us. In this way, we keep our self-construct going. Yet, in spite of all this self-generating activity, there may still be no sense of enduring stability in one's own being or calmness in the mind. Buddhists might say that this is because there is no absolute separate "self" in the first place, just the process of a continually self-constructing narrative: in other words, "selfing." If we could only recognize the process of selfing as an ingrained habit and then give ourselves permission to take the day off, to stop trying so hard to be "somebody" and instead just experience being itself, perhaps we would be a lot happier and more relaxed.

This doesn't mean, by the way, that "you have to be a somebody before you can be a nobody," by which is meant that you should have a robust sense of self before you explore the essentially empty nature of the personal pronouns. Because when the term "not-self" is being used, it does not mean being a nobody. What it means is that everything is interdependent and that there is no isolated, independent core "you." You are only you in relationship to all other forces and events in the world—including your ancestors, known and unknown, your parents, your childhood, what is going on at the molecular and cellular levels in the trillions of cells that constitute your body, your thoughts and feelings, outside events, time, and so on. Moreover, you are already a somebody, no matter what. You are who you already are. But who you are is not your name, your age, your childhood, your beliefs, your fears. They are part of it, but not the whole. They only define you if you want them to or let them. You are not your narrative. You are not the story of you that you tell yourself, whatever it is. You are so much larger than the narrative, than any narrative.

So, when we speak about not trying so hard to be "somebody" and instead just directly experiencing this moment directly, what it means is that you start from where you find yourself and work here. Meditation is not about trying to dissolve your personhood or become a nobody or a contemplative zombie, incapable of living in the real world and facing real problems. It's about seeing things as they are, without the distortions of our own thought processes. Part of that is perceiving that everything is interconnected and that while our conventional sense of "having" a self is helpful in many ways, it is not absolutely real or solid or permanent. So, if you stop trying to make yourself into more than you are out of fear that you are less than you are, whoever you really are will be a lot lighter and happier—and easier to live with too.

We might begin by taking things a little less personally. When something happens, try to see it without the self-orientation, just for fun. Maybe it just happened. Maybe it's not aimed at you. Watch your mind at such times. Is it getting into "I" this and "me" that? Ask yourself, "Who am I?" or "What is this 'I' that is claiming ownership?"

Awareness itself can help balance out the selfing and reduce its impact. Notice, too, that whatever we mean by self is impermanent. Whatever you try to hold on to that has to do with yourself eludes you. It can't be held because it is constantly changing, decaying, and being reconstructed again, always slightly differently, depending on the circumstances of the moment. This makes the sense of self what is called in chaos theory a "strange attractor," a pattern that has a signature dynamical shape and order to it yet is simultaneously ever changing and unpredictably disordered. And it never repeats itself. Whenever you look, it is slightly different.

The elusive nature of a concrete, permanent, unchanging self is quite a hopeful observation. It means that you can stop taking yourself so damn seriously and get out from under the pressures of having the details of your personal life be central to the operation of the universe. By recognizing and letting go of selfing impulses whenever they arise, and of the self-centered narratives they conjure up—in other words, by recognizing the essentially empty and impersonal nature of those impulses—we accord the universe a little more room to make things happen and accord significantly more degrees of freedom for ourselves in any and every moment. But since we are intimately enfolded into that universe and participate in its unfolding, the danger is that it will defer in the face of too much self-centered, self-indulgent, self-critical, self-insecure, self-anxious activity on our part and arrange for the dreamworld of our self-oriented thinking to look and feel only too real. If we see it for what it is in any moment, the self-fabricated phantom collapses instantly, like a soap bubble when touched by a finger.

Anger Flashback

The look of utter despair and silent pleading for me not to get angry etched into my daughter's eleven-year-old face as I got out of the car at her friend's house early one Sunday morning, decades ago and still fresh in my mind, does penetrate my awareness, but not completely enough to rein in the annoyance and anger she sees rising in me, who she fears will make a scene and embarrass her. I am feeling too much momentum in this moment to stop completely, although later I would wish I had. I wished that I had let her look stop me in that moment, touch me, turn me toward seeing what was really important—namely, that she feel that she could depend on me and trust me rather than fear that I would betray her or mortify her emerging social sensitivity. But in that moment, I was too upset about feeling manipulated by her friend, who was supposed to be ready at a certain time and wasn't, to fully appreciate my daughter's social discomfort.

I am caught up in an eddy of self-righteous indignation. My "I" does not want to be kept waiting, to be taken advantage of. I reassure her that I will not make a scene but that I also want to communicate about it right now because I am feeling used. I make early morning inquiries, tinged with annoyance, of her sleepy mother, then wait, inwardly fuming, for what turns out to be a remarkably short time—another narrative that turned out to be off and totally gratuitous on my part.

And so the matter dissolved. But not in my memory, which still carries, and I hope always will, that look on my daughter's face that I was unable to read quickly enough to be fully present for. Had I been able to, the anger would have died then and there.

There is a price we pay for being attached to a narrow view of being "right" and the selfing behind it. My passing mood state is far less important to me than my daughter's trust. But in that moment, her trust got trampled all the same. Without care and awareness, small-minded feeling states can dominate the moment. It happens all the time. The collective pain we cause others—often the ones we love the most—as well as ourselves, is so unnecessary. And it lingers. Hard as it is for us to admit, especially about ourselves, anger arising from impulses to protect our unfounded and unexamined insecurities may be something we indulge in and surrender to far too often.

Cat-Food Lessons

We haven't had cats for decades in our family, but I am letting this stand as an example of how easy it is to get fixated on having to have things a certain way—my way—and the value of realizing that my way is not the only way, that people see the same thing very, very differently, whether it is the condition of the kitchen sink, or how to load a dishwasher, or how to approach any particular task or encounter.

I hate finding caked cat dishes in the kitchen sink along with ours. I'm not sure why this pushes my buttons so strongly, but it does. Perhaps it comes from not having had a pet when I was growing up. Or maybe I think it's a public health threat (you know, viruses and the like). When I choose to clean the cats' bowls, I first clean the whole sink of our dishes, then I wash theirs. Anyway, I don't like it when I find dirty cat dishes in the sink, and I react right away when I do.

First I get angry. Then the anger gets more personal, and I find myself directing it at whoever I think is the culprit, which is usually my wife, Myla. I feel hurt because she doesn't respect my feelings. I tell her on countless occasions that I don't like it, that it disgusts me. I've asked her as politely as I know how not to do it, but she often does it anyway. She thinks I'm being silly and compulsive, and when she's pressed for time, she just leaves the caked cat dishes soaking in the sink.

My discovery of cat dishes in the sink can quickly escalate to a heated dispute, mostly because I am feeling angry and hurt and above all justified in "my" anger, "my" hurt, because I know "I" am right. Cat dishes shouldn't be in the sink! But when they are, the selfing on my part can get rather strong.

Over time, I came to notice that I am not getting so bent out of shape about this anymore. I didn't specifically try to change how I'm dealing with it. I still feel the same about the cat food, but somehow, I'm seeing the whole thing differently too, with greater awareness and with much more of a sense of humor. For one, when it happens now—and it still does with annoying frequency—I find that I am aware of my reaction the moment it happens, and I look at it. "This is it," I remind myself!

I observe the anger as it starts rising in me. It turns out that it is preceded by a mild feeling of revulsion. Then I notice the stirrings of a feeling of betrayal, which is not so mild. Someone in my family didn't respect my request, and I am taking it very personally. After all, my feelings count in the family, don't they?

I have taken to experimenting with my reactions at the kitchen sink by watching them very closely without acting on them. I can report that the initial feeling of revulsion is not all that bad, and if I stay with it, breathe with it, and permit myself to just feel it, it actually goes away within a second or two. I have also noticed that it is the sense of betrayal, of being thwarted in my wishes, that makes me mad much more than the cat food itself. So, I discover, it's not really the cat food that is the source of my anger. It's that I'm not feeling listened to and respected. Very different from the cat food. A-ha!

Then I remember that my wife and kids see this whole thing very differently. They think I am making a big deal out of nothing, and that while they will try to respect my wishes when it feels reasonable to them, at other times it doesn't and they just do it anyway, maybe even without thinking about me at all.

So I've stopped taking it personally. When I really don't want caked cat food dishes in the sink, I roll up my sleeves and I clean the dishes in that moment, all of them. Otherwise, I just leave them there and go away. We no longer have fights about it. In fact, I find myself smiling now when I do come across the offending objects in the sink. After all, they have taught me a lot.

TRY: Watching your reactions in idiosyncratic situations that particularly annoy you or make you feel angry or self-righteous. Notice how even speaking of something "making" you angry surrenders your agency and power to others. Do you really want to do that? Such occasions are good opportunities to experiment with mindfulness as a pot into which you can put all your feelings and just be with them, letting them slowly cook, or even boil, reminding yourself that you don't have to do anything with them right away, that they will become more cooked, more easily metabolized, and therefore digested and integrated into a deeper understanding of things simply by letting them simmer in the pot of mindfulness or, put differently, the embrace of awareness.

Observe the ways in which your feelings are creations of your mind's view of things, and that that view may not be—in fact, cannot be—complete. Can you allow whatever state of affairs that so effectively winds up triggering mindless self-righteousness and reactivity in you to be okay for now and simply hold it in awareness, making yourself neither right nor wrong? Can you be patient enough and courageous enough to explore putting stronger and stronger emotions into the pot, containing them for a time and just letting them cook, rather than projecting them outward and forcing the world to be as you want it to be when you get caught in a moment of contraction? Can you see how such a simple but not easy practice might lead to knowing yourself in new ways, and freeing yourself from at least some old, worn-out, limiting views and from idiosyncratic, self-privileging attachments that disregard and alienate those who may see and feel things very differently?

Parenting as Practice

I took up meditating when I was in my early twenties. In those days, I had some flexibility in terms of my time and was able to periodically attend meditation retreats lasting ten days or two weeks. These retreats were designed so that the participants could devote each day from early morning to late at night solely to mindful sitting and walking, with a few hearty vegetarian meals thrown in, all in silence. We were supported in this inner work by excellent meditation teachers, who would give inspiring talks in the evening to help us deepen and broaden our practice, and who would see us every so often for individual interviews to check on how things were going.

I loved these retreats because they enabled me to put everything else in my life on hold, go off someplace pleasant and peaceful in the countryside, get taken care of, and live an extremely simplified contemplative life, where the only real agenda was to practice, practice, practice.

Not that it was easy, mind you. There was often a lot of physical pain just from sitting still for that many hours, and that was nothing compared to the emotional pain that would sometimes surface as the mind and body became more still and less busy.

When my wife and I decided to have children, I knew that I would have to give up the retreats, at least for some time. I said to myself that I could always return to the contemplative setting when my children had grown up enough not to need me around all the time. There was a certain romantic touch to the fantasy of returning to the monastic life as an old man. The prospect of giving up these retreats, or at least cutting back on them a lot, didn't bother me too much because, much as I valued them, I had decided that there was a way to look at having children as a meditation retreat in its own right—one that would have most of the important features of those I was giving up, except for the quiet and the simplicity.

This was how I saw it: You could look at each baby as a little Buddha or Zen master, your own private mindfulness teacher, parachuted into your life, whose presence and actions were guaranteed to push every button and challenge every belief and limit you had, giving you continual opportunities to see where you were attached to something and to let go of it. For each child, it would be at least an eighteen-year retreat with very little, if any, time off. The retreat schedule would be relentless and require frequent acts of selflessness and lovingkindness. My life, which up to that time basically consisted of looking after my own personal needs and desires, perfectly normal for a young single person, was about to change profoundly. Becoming a parent clearly was going to be the biggest transformation of my adult life up to that point. To do it well would demand the greatest clarity of view and the greatest letting go and letting be I had ever been challenged with.

For one, babies invite and require attending to constantly. Their needs must be met on their schedule, not yours, and every day, not just when you feel like it. Most importantly, babies and children require your full presence in order to thrive and grow. They need to be held, the more the better, walked with, sung to, rocked, played with, comforted, sometimes nurtured late at night or early in the morning when you are feeling depleted, exhausted, and only want to sleep, or when you have pressing obligations and responsibilities elsewhere. The deep and constantly changing needs of children are all perfect opportunities for parents to be fully present rather than to operate in the autopilot mode, to relate consciously rather than mechanically, to sense the being in each child and let his or her vibrancy, vitality, and purity call forth our own. I believed that parenting was nothing short of a perfect opportunity to deepen mindfulness if I could let the children and the family become my teachers, and remember to recognize and listen carefully to the lessons in living that would be coming fast and furiously.

Like any long retreat, there have been easy periods and harder periods, wonderful moments and deeply painful ones. Through it all, the principle of looking at it as a meditation retreat and honoring the children and the family situation as my teachers has proven its primacy and value time and time again. Parenting is a high-pressure job situation. In the early years, it seems like a full-time job for about ten people, and usually there are only two, or even one, to do it all, and no manual that comes with the babies telling you how to proceed. It is the hardest job in the world to do well, and much of the time you don't even know if you are, or even what that might mean. And most of us get virtually no preparation or training for parenting, only on-the-job, moment-to-moment training, as things unfold.

At the beginning, there are precious few opportunities for respite. The job calls for you to be continually engaged. And the children are always pushing your limits to find out about the world and about who they are. What's more, as they grow and develop, they change. No sooner have you figured out how to relate well to one situation than they grow out of that and into something you've never seen before. You have to be continually mindful and present so that you aren't lingering with a view of things that no longer applies. And, of course, there are no stock answers or simple formulas for how to do things "right" in the world of parenting. This means you are unavoidably in creative and challenging situations almost all the time and, at the same time, faced with a lot of repetitive tasks you do over and over, again and again and again.

And it gets more challenging as the children grow older and develop their own ideas and strong wills. It's one thing to look after the needs of babies, which are very simple, after all, especially before they can talk and when they are most adorable. It's quite another to see clearly and to respond effectively and with some modicum of wisdom and balance (after all, you are the adult) when there is a continual clash of wills with older children, who are not always so cute and cuddly, who can argue circles around you, tease each other mercilessly, fight, rebel, refuse to listen, get into social situations in which they need your guidance and clarity but may not be open to it; in short, whose needs require an ongoing emotional attentiveness that at times can leave you feeling there is little time for yourself. The list of situations in which your equanimity and clarity will be sorely challenged and you will find yourself "losing it" is endless. There is simply no escape, no hiding, no dissimilation that will serve either them or you. Your children will see it all from the inside and up close: your foibles, idiosyncrasies, warts, and pimples, your shortcomings, your inconsistencies, and your failures.

These trials are not impediments to either parenting or mindfulness practice. They are the practice, if you can remember to see it this way. Otherwise, your life as a parent can become one very long and unsatisfying burden, in which your lack of strength and clarity of purpose may lead to forgetting to honor or even to see the inner goodness of your children and yourself. Children can easily become wounded and diminished from a childhood that consistently fails to adequately honor their needs or recognize their inner beauty. Wounding will just create more problems for them and for the family, problems with self-confidence and self-esteem, with communication and competencies, problems that don't necessarily disappear on their own as the children grow older. And as parents, we may not be open enough to perceive the signs of this diminishment or wounding and then be able to act to heal it because it may have come in some measure through our own hands or through our cluelessness, our own lack of awareness of what might be going on beneath the surface behaviors. Also, such indicators may be subtle, easily denied, or attributable to other causes, thus freeing us in our own minds from a responsibility that may be truly ours to assume.

It is obvious that, with all that energy going outward, there has to be some source of energy coming in that nurtures and revitalizes the parents from time to time, or the process itself will not be sustainable for long. Where might this energy come from? I can think of only two possible sources: outside support from a partner, other family members, friends, babysitters, community, and so on and from doing other things you love, at least occasionally; and inner support, which can of course take many forms, but in this context, an important source might derive from formal meditation practice if you can make even a little time in your life for stillness, for just being, for just sitting or doing a little yoga, for nourishing yourself in ways that you need to be nourished.

I meditate early in the morning because I love the quiet before things start to stir in the outer world. That custom came in handy when I was a young parent, as there was really no other time when things were quiet in the house and nobody was demanding my attention—and also because, what with work and other obligations, if I didn't devote major time to formal practice in the early morning, I might have been too tired or too busy to get to it later. Of course, practicing in the early morning has the extra benefit of powerfully setting the tone for the entire day. It is both a reminder and an affirmation of what is most important and makes it more likely that mindfulness will naturally spill out into other aspects of the day.

But when we had babies in the house, even the morning time was up for grabs. You couldn't be too attached to anything because everything you set out to do, even if you arranged it very carefully, was always getting interrupted or completely thwarted. Our babies slept very little. They always seemed to be up late and to wake up early, especially if I was meditating. They seemed to sense when I was up and would wake up too. Some days I would have to push my time for myself back to 4:00 a.m. to get any sitting or yoga in. At other times I was just too exhausted to care and figured the sleep was more important anyway. And sometimes I would just sit with the baby on my lap, and let them decide how long it would last. They loved being wrapped up in the meditation blanket, with only their heads sticking out, and frequently would stay still for extended periods, while I held not my breathing but our breathing in awareness.

I felt strongly in those days, and still do, that an awareness of my body and my breath and of our close contact as I held them while we sat helped our babies to sense calmness and explore stillness and feelings of acceptance. And their inner relaxation, which was much greater and purer than mine because their minds were not filled with adult thoughts and worries, helped me to be calmer and more relaxed and present. When they were toddlers, I would do yoga with them climbing up, riding on, or hanging from my body. In playing around on the floor, we would spontaneously discover new yoga postures for two bodies, things that we could do together. A mostly nonverbal, mindful, and respectful body-play of this sort was a source of tremendous fun and joy for me as a father and a deep source of connectedness that we all shared in.

The older children get, the harder it is to remember that they are still live-in Zen masters. The "curriculum" gets more and more complex and challenging, and with it, the challenges to be mindful and nonreactive, and the need to look clearly at my reactions and overreactions and to own when I am off seems to get greater as I gradually have less and less direct say in their lives. Old tapes from my own upbringing seem to surface with the volume on full blast before I know what is happening. Archetypal male stuff, about my role in the family, legitimate and illegitimate authority and how to assert my power, how comfortable I feel in the house, interpersonal relationships among people of very different ages and stages and their oft-competing needs. Each day is a new challenge. Often it feels overwhelming and sometimes quite lonely. You sense widening gulfs and recognize the importance of distance for healthy psychic development and exploration, but the moving apart, healthy as it may be, also hurts. Sometimes I forget what it means to be an adult myself and get stuck in infantile behaviors. The kids quickly straighten me out and wake me up again if my own mindfulness is not up to the task at that moment.

Parenting and family life can be a perfect field for mindfulness practice, but it's not for the weak-hearted, the selfish or lazy, or the hopelessly romantic. Parenting is a mirror that forces you to look at yourself. If you can learn from what you observe, you just may have a chance to keep growing.

*

Once the realization is accepted that even between the closest human beings infinite distances continue to exist, a wonderful living side by side can grow up, if they succeed in loving the distance between them which makes it possible for each to see the other whole against the sky.

RAINER MARIA RILKE, *Letters*

*

The attainment of wholeness requires one to stake one's whole being. Nothing less will do; there can be no easier conditions, no substitutes, no compromises.

C. G. JUNG

TRY: If you are a parent or grandparent, try seeing the children as your teachers. Observe them in silence at times if you can do it unobtrusively. Listen more carefully to their energies, what speaks to them and what doesn't. Learn to read their body language. Watch how they carry themselves in the moment, what they draw (and what they want to tell you about their drawing or painting, or anything else they do), what they see, how they behave, what they love. What are their needs in this moment? At this time in the arc of their day? At this stage in their lives? Ask yourself, "How can I best serve them right now?" It could very well be to just leave them be—the exact opposite of so-called helicopter parenting. Follow what your heart tells you. And remember, advice is probably the last thing that will be useful in most situations, unless it is just the right moment for it and you are very sensitive to the timing and how you frame things. Just being yourself and being fully present, open and available but not overbearing, is the greatest gift of all for them. And mindful hugging from time to time doesn't hurt, either.

Parenting Two

Of course, for a major stretch of your lifetime, you are your children's major life teacher as much as they are your teachers. How you take on this role will make a big difference in their lives as well as in your own. I see parenting as extended but temporary guardianship. If we think of them in too constrained a way as "our" children, or "my" children, and start relating to them as ours to shape and control to satisfy our own needs, we are, I believe, in deep trouble. Children are and will always be their own beings, born to their own time. But they do need great love and guidance to come into the fullness of who they are within the world they will inherit, far different from ours, given the current revolutionary challenges of the present era and imaginable futures. Parents and other caretakers need wisdom and patience in abundance to pass on what is most important to the generation coming along the path. Some—me included—need virtually constant mindfulness in addition to our basic instincts for nurturing and loving and kindness to do this job well, protecting them as best we can as they develop their own strengths, views, and skills for moving along the paths they will later explore more fully on their own.

Some people who find meditation valuable in their own lives are sorely tempted to teach their children to meditate. This could be a big mistake, depending on your motivation and your approach. To my mind, the best way to impart wisdom, meditation, or anything else to your children, especially when they are young, is to live it yourself, embody what you most want to impart, and keep your mouth shut. The more you talk about meditation or extol it or insist that your children do things a certain way, the more likely you are, I think, to turn them off to it, perhaps for life. They will sense your strong attachment to your view of things and the desire behind promoting certain beliefs that are only your own and not their truths, and they will instinctively know that this is not their path but yours.

If you are devoted to your own meditation practice and find it beneficial in various ways, your children will witness that firsthand and accept it matter-of-factly, as part of life, a normal activity. They may even sometimes be drawn to imitate you, as they do with most other things parents do. The point is, the motivation to learn meditation and to practice should for the most part originate with them and be pursued only to the degree that they maintain interest in it themselves.

The real teaching and transmission, to the degree there is any transmission at all, is almost entirely nonverbal. My children would sometimes join me in practicing yoga because they saw me doing it and it looked like fun. But most of the time they had more important things to do and little interest in it. The same was true for sitting meditation. They knew about it, and when they wanted to, they knew how to sit from sitting in my lap when they were little.

If you practice yourself, you will discover certain times when it may be sensible to make meditative recommendations to your children. These suggestions may or may not "work" at the time, but they can be a kind of planting seeds for later. Good occasions are when your children are experiencing pain or fear or are having a hard time letting go into sleep. Without being overbearing or insistent, you can suggest that they tune in to their breathing, slow it down, float on the waves in a little boat, describe the fear or the pain with color or images or locations in the body, and use their imagination to explore and "play" with the situation. They can then remind themselves that the feelings and thoughts they are having are just like pictures in the mind, like video or a movie. They can play with changing the channel, the video, the movie, the thought, the image, the color, and sometimes discover that they might feel better more quickly and more in control.

Sometimes this works well with preschoolers, but they can get embarrassed or think it's silly once they get to be around six or seven. Then this too passes, and they become receptive again at certain times. In any event, seeds have been planted suggesting that there are simple ways to use one's attention to work with fear and pain. Often children will come back to this knowledge when they are older. They will know from direct experience that they are more than just their thoughts and feelings, and have the capacity to relate to them in ways that give them more choices to participate in and influence the outcomes of various situations. As one fifth-grader put it to her stressed-out mother: "Just because other people's minds are waving doesn't mean that your mind has to wave too."

Myla and I wrote a book on mindful parenting, *Everyday Blessings*, published in 1997, revised in 2013. As grandparents now, the beat very much goes on.

Some Pitfalls Along the Path

If you follow the lifelong path of mindfulness as both a regular formal daily meditation practice and as a Way of being in relationship to life in all moments, the biggest potential obstacle at points along your journey will undoubtedly be your thinking mind.

For instance, you might come to think from time to time that you are "getting somewhere" in your meditation practice, especially if you have had some satisfying moments that transcend what you have experienced before. Then you might go around thinking, maybe even saying, that you have gotten somewhere, that the meditation practice really "works." The ego, the selfing impulse, wants to lay claim to and take credit for this special feeling or understanding, whatever it is. As soon as this happens, you are no longer into meditation but into advertising. It is easy to get caught here, using meditation practice to support the self-inflation habit.

As soon as you're caught, you cease seeing clearly. Even a clear insight, once it is claimed by this kind of self-serving thinking, rapidly clouds over and loses its authenticity. So you have to remind yourself that all colorations of "I," "me," and "mine" are just eddies and whirlpools in the stream of thinking that are liable to catch you up for a time and carry you away from your own heart and the actuality—the each-ness and suchness—of direct experience. This reminder keeps the practice alive for us at the very moments we may need it the most and are most ready to betray it. It keeps us looking deeply, in the spirit of inquiry and genuine curiosity, and asking constantly, "What is this?" "What is this?"

Or perhaps, on occasion you may find yourself thinking that you're getting nowhere with your meditation practice. Noth-ing that you want to happen has happened. There is a sense of staleness, of boredom. Here again, it's the thinking that's the problem. There is nothing wrong with feelings of boredom or staleness, or of not getting anywhere, just as there is noth-ing wrong with feeling that you are getting somewhere, and in fact, your practice may well be showing signs of deepening and becoming more robust. The pitfall is when you inflate such experiences or thoughts and you start believing in them as special. It's when you get attached to your experience that the practice arrests, and your development along with it. Seung Sahn used to say, "Open your mouth and you're wrong."

TRY: Whenever you find yourself thinking you are getting somewhere or that you're not getting where you are supposed to be, it can be helpful to ask yourself things like, "Where am I supposed to get?" "Who is supposed to get somewhere?" "Why are some mind states less valid to observe and accept as being present than others?" "Am I inviting mindfulness into each moment, or indulging in mindless repetition of the forms of meditation practice, mistaking the form for the essence of it?" "Am I reducing meditation to a mechanical technique or seeing it as a Way of being?"

These questions can help you cut through those moments when self-involved feeling states, mindless habits, and strong emotions dominate your practice. They can quickly bring you back to the freshness and beauty of each moment as it is. Perhaps you forgot or didn't quite grasp that meditation really is the one human activity in which you are not trying to get anywhere else but simply allowing yourself to be where and as you already are. This is a bitter medicine to swallow when you don't like what is happening or where you find yourself, but it is especially worth swallowing at such times.

Is Mindfulness Spiritual?

If you look up the word "spirit" in the dictionary, you will find that it comes from the Latin, *spirare*, meaning "to breathe." The inbreath is inspiration; the outbreath, expiration. From these come all the associations of spirit with the breath of life, vital energy, consciousness, the soul, often framed as divine gifts bestowed upon us and therefore an aspect of the holy, the numinous, the ineffable. In the deepest sense, the breath itself is the ultimate gift of spirit. But, as we have seen, the depth and range of its virtues can remain unknown to us as long as our attention is absorbed elsewhere. The cultivation of mindfulness is constantly reminding us of that vitality in every moment that we have. In wakefulness, everything inspires. Nothing is excluded from the domain of spirit.

As much as I can, I avoid using the word "spiritual" altogether. I never found it particularly useful or necessary, or appropriate in our work at the hospital bringing mindfulness into the mainstream of medicine and health care over the decades through MBSR. Nor was it useful in most other settings in which we worked, such as our multiethnic inner-city MBSR clinic, prisons, schools, businesses, nor in training collegiate, Olympic, and professional athletes. Nor do I find the word "spiritual" particularly congenial to the way I hold the tending and nurturing of my own meditation practice.

This is not to deny that meditation can be thought of fundamentally as a "spiritual practice." It's just that I have a problem with the inaccurate, incomplete, and frequently misguided connotations of that word. Of course, meditation has to do with waking up to our true nature as sentient beings and learning how to embody wakefulness and heartfulness in all aspects of our lives. It can be a profound path for discovering and taking up residency, so to speak, in our truest nature as unique human beings. That said, for me, the vocabulary of spirituality often creates more practical problems than it solves.

In the early eighties, Roger Walsh published a paper referring to meditation as a "consciousness discipline." I prefer that formulation to the term "spiritual practice" because the word "spiritual" evokes such different connotations in different people. Those connotations are unavoidably entwined in belief systems and unconscious expectations that most of us are reluctant to examine and that can all too easily prevent us from developing or even from hearing that genuine growth and embodied realization are possible.

Over the years, people would come up to me in the hospital and tell me that their time in the MBSR program was the most spiritual experience they ever had. I was happy that they felt that way because it was coming directly out of their own experience with the meditation practice, and not from some theory or ideology or belief system. I usually felt that I knew what they meant. But I also knew that they were trying to put words to an inward experience that is ultimately beyond words and labels. Whatever their experience or insight was, my deepest hope was that it would take root, stay alive, grow. If it is truly taken in that the practice is not about getting anywhere else, not even to pleasant or profound "spiritual" experiences, but an invitation to open to the actuality of things as they are in this moment, pleasant, unpleasant, or neither, and perhaps taste a moment of equanimity in resting in awareness in the timelessness of this moment, I rest content. Hopefully, they will come to understand that mindfulness is beyond all thinking, wishful and otherwise, that the here and now is the stage on which this ongoing mysterious adventure we call life unfolds continuously.

From this vantage point, the concept of spirituality can narrow our thinking rather than extend it. All too commonly, some things are thought of as spiritual while others are excluded. Is science spiritual? Is being a parent spiritual? Are dogs and cats spiritual? What about other animals? Nature? Is the body spiritual? Is the mind spiritual? Is childbirth? Is eating? Is painting, or playing music, or taking a walk, or looking at a flower? Is breathing spiritual, or climbing a mountain? Obviously, it all depends on how you encounter it, how you hold it in awareness, how you apprehend the world.

Mindfulness allows everything to shine with the luminosity that the word "spiritual" is meant to connote. Einstein spoke of "that cosmic religious feeling" he experienced contemplating the underlying order and mystery of the physical universe. The great geneticist Barbara McClintock, whose research was both ignored and disdained by her male colleagues for decades until it was finally recognized at age eighty with a Nobel Prize, spoke of "a feeling for the organism" in her efforts to unravel and understand the intricacies of corn genetics. Perhaps ultimately, "spiritual" simply means experiencing wholeness and interconnectedness directly, a seeing that individuality and the totality are interwoven, that nothing is separate or extraneous. If you see in this way, then everything becomes spiritual in its deepest sense. Doing science is spiritual. The James Webb Space Telescope and what it is showing us of the universe is only one of an infinite number of examples. And so is washing the dishes. It is the inner experience that counts. And you have to be here for it. All else is mere thinking.

At the same time, it is good to be on the lookout for tendencies toward self-deception, deluded thinking, grandiosity, self-inflation, and exploitation and cruelty directed at other beings. A lot of harm has come in all eras from people attached to one view of spiritual "truth." And a lot more has come from people who hide behind the cloak of spirituality and are willing to harm others—often in horrific ways—to feed their own appetites.

Moreover, our ideas of spirituality frequently ring with a slightly holier-than-thou resonance to the attuned ear. Narrow, literalist views of spirit often place it above the "gross," "polluted," "deluded" domain of body, mind, and matter. Falling into such views, people can use ideas of spirit to run from life.

From a mythological perspective, the notion of spirit has an upwardly rising quality, as Carl Jung, James Hillman, Robert Bly, and other proponents of archetypal psychology have pointed out. The energy of spirit embodies ascent, a rising above the earthbound qualities of this world to a world of the nonmaterial, filled with light and radiance, a world beyond opposites, where everything merges into oneness, nirvana, heaven, a cosmic unity. But although unity is surely an all-too-rare human experience, it is not the end of the story. What is more, all too often it is merely nine parts wishful thinking (but thinking nonetheless) and only one part direct experience. The quest for spiritual unity, especially in youth, is often driven by naiveté and a romantic yearning to transcend the pain, the suffering, and the responsibilities of this world of eachness and suchness, which includes the moist and the dark.

The *idea* of transcendence—not transcendence itself—can be a great escape, a high-octane fuel for delusion. This is why the Buddhist tradition, especially Zen, emphasizes coming full circle, back to the ordinary and the everyday, what they call "being free and easy in the marketplace." This means being grounded anywhere and everywhere, in any circumstances, neither above nor below, simply present but fully present—awake and aware in the unique constellation of form and emptiness that is you. Zen practitioners have the wholly irreverent and wonderfully provocative saying, "If you meet the Buddha on the road, kill him," which means that any conceptual attachments to Buddha or enlightenment are far from the mark.

Notice that the mountain image as we use it in the mountain meditation is not merely the loftiness of the peak, high above all the "baseness" of quotidian living. It is also the groundedness of the base, rooted in rock, a willingness to sit and be with all conditions, such as fog, rain, snow, and cold or, in terms of the mind, loneliness, depression, fear, anger, confusion, pain, and suffering.

Rock, the students of psyche remind us, is symbolic of soul rather than spirit. Its direction is downward, the soul journey a symbolic descent, a going underground. Water, too, is symbolic of soul, embodying the downward element, as in the lake meditation, pooling in the low places, cradled in rock, dark and mysterious, receptive, often cold and damp.

The soul feeling is rooted in multiplicity rather than oneness, grounded in complexity and ambiguity, eachness and suchness, individuality and diversity. Soul stories are stories of the quest, of risking one's life, of enduring darkness and encountering shadows, of being buried underground or underwater, of being lost and at times confused but persevering nevertheless. Tolkien comes immediately to mind. In persevering, we ultimately come in touch with our own goldenness as we emerge from the darkness and the submerged gloom of the underground that we most feared but nevertheless faced. This goldenness was always ours, is always with us, but hidden. It has to be discovered anew at various stages of life, through descent into darkness and grief. It is ours even if it remains unseen by others or even at times by us ourselves. It might be called our true or truest nature.

Fairy tales in all cultures are for the most part soul stories rather than spirit stories. The dwarf is a soul figure, as we saw in "The Water of Life." "Cinderella" is a soul story. The archetype there is ashes, as Robert Bly pointed out in *Iron John*. You (because these stories are all about you) are kept down, in the ashes, close to the hearth, grounded but also grieving, your inner beauty unperceived and exploited. During this time, inwardly, a new development is taking place, a maturation, a metamorphosis, a tempering, which culminates in the emergence of a fully developed human being, radiant and golden but also wise to the ways of the world, no longer a passive and naive agent. The fully developed human being embodies the unity of soul and spirit, up and down, material and nonmaterial.

The meditation practice itself is itself both a mirror and a catalyst of this journey of human growth and development. It too takes us down as well as up, demands that we face, even embrace, pain and darkness as well as joy and light. It reminds us to use whatever comes up and wherever we find ourselves as occasions for inquiry, for opening, for growing in strength and wisdom, for *forging our own path in walking*, as Francisco Varela liked to say, a nice metaphor for mindfulness practice as a way of being.

For me, words like "soul" and "spirit" are attempts to describe the inner experience of human beings as we seek to know ourselves and find our place in this strange and ever-more-rapidly-changing world. No truly spiritual work could be lacking in soul, nor can any truly soulful work be devoid of spirit. Our demons, our dragons, our dwarfs, our witches and ogres, our princes and princesses, our kings and queens, our dungeons, crevices, and grails, our oars to drive our ship in youth or to plant in the ground in old age are all here now, ready to teach us and serve us. But we have to listen closely, and take them on in the spirit of the heroic, never-ending quest each of us embodies, for what it means to be fully human. Perhaps the most "spiritual" thing any of us can do is simply to look through our own eyes, see with eyes of wholeness, and act with integrity and kindness.

*

. . . their eyes, their ancient glittering eyes, are gay.

W. B. YEATS, "Lapis Lazuli"

Afterword

I don't imagine people buy books about meditation all that casually. The fact that this one has now been in print for thirty years in more than forty languages suggests that people are drawn to and touched by its basic message. Perhaps that is because we are so starved for our own direct experience of being who we somehow know deep down we already are but perhaps feel slightly at a distance from all the same. Perhaps it and an ever-increasing number of wonderful Dharma teachings for our age are tapping an increasingly wide-spread and deep yearning for authenticity, intimacy, and clarity and reminding us of what we already know: that these qualities can be found only within ourselves and within the unfolding of our direct experience of living, and that unfolding is always and only here, and always and only now, whatever our circumstances. Perhaps people recognize in the title the calling to wake up to our experience while we have the chance, and how easy it is to sleepwalk through and therefore miss much of our life, telling ourselves nice or not-so-nice stories about who we are and where we are going, pursuing perhaps some deluded fantasy there is little likelihood we will ever actualize and from which we might never recover were it to come about.

This book was so close to my heart and felt so complete to me that, when asked to write something for a tenth-anniversary edition, I found myself reluctant to introduce new material at the beginning. Hence this afterword, now reworked for this edition another twenty years on. And with that ensuing time, no question that a new introduction was appropriate as well.

I also came to see that perhaps some of what I thought was appropriate to include in the original book might have only limited resonance for readers decades later, given the passage of time and how rapidly the world is changing. Still, I chose to keep the original text pretty much the way it was—fairy tales, young parenting stories, pronouncements on spirituality, and all—lightly reshaped as best I could with the benefit of time and practice but, still, basically the book that it was from the beginning.

*

If you have made it this far in our journey together, there is still much to say—the Dharma being infinite—and, at the same time, nothing more that needs saying. The meditation practice itself is timeless. It is deeply gratifying to see how broadly and deeply it has taken root in mainstream circles around the world, especially at a time of such great inner and outer turmoil, confusion, and existential threats to humanity and the biosphere: wanton wars of cruelty and utter devastation; ever-accelerating eco-destruction; ferocious time acceleration driven by the advent of the digital age; the looming promise and potential terrifying consequences for humanity as we know it of attempts at developing AGI without a clear understanding of their risks; the wonders and the dangers stemming from the interconnectedness of the internet feeding our tendency to want to get more and more done in less and less time;

the lure and dangers of getting lost in social media, where maximizing "engagement" rules the algorithms, no matter what the downstream costs from rabbit holes, alternative facts, and deepfakes, where nothing is what it seems, addictions of all kinds that have ever-more-destructive effects on our youth, their mental health and their sense of intrinsic worthiness and belonging. All these disruptive arisings, most unimaginable thirty years ago, are putting us at risk of losing the potential to tap into our full capabilities and genius stemming from 3.5 billion years of entirely *analog* evolution in this less-than-tiny corner of the universe that gave rise to us and to human sentience—before we even recognize, never mind learn how to tap into, our full biological human genius in the service of peace, tranquility, wisdom, wellbeing, and love. With every day and with every upgrade, we may be more and more digitally connected through our devices and social media, while unwittingly losing essential connectivity with ourselves, with our bodies and brains, with our minds and our hearts, with each other, and with the natural world on this still-Goldilocks—not too hot and not too cold (but for how long?)—planet. We are increasingly distracted or besotted, running an ever-greater risk of never being present with and for ourselves, of losing touch almost entirely with the domain of being. Nothing like this has ever been seen in the history of humanity. The species itself is at a critical juncture, a tipping point, and mindfulness, our innate capacity for wakefulness and openhearted presence, for clear seeing, for wisdom and compassion, has never been more critically important if we are to individually and collectively navigate challenges of this magnitude and those still to come.

To my mind, what we need, now more than ever, within all the turmoil, is what I call an orthogonal rotation in consciousness* to accompany and shape the trajectory of our various engagements and entanglements in the world, as well as to guide us individually and collectively in the full development of our potential as human beings, especially at the analog/digital interface. Mindfulness meditation, especially when it is understood as a way of being—as living life as if it really mattered, moment by moment by moment, rather than merely as a technique or as one more thing you have to do during your already too-busy day—is one powerful vehicle for realizing such transformative and healing possibilities in ourselves and in the world. And because it is a door into the timeless, it operates beyond time and underneath time, as well as inside time, and so allows for transformation without having to strive to get anywhere else or beat oneself up along the way for being inadequate or imperfect.

For, as this book and the meditation practice itself affirms and confirms, when you drop in on the present moment, you are already perfect. We all are. Perfectly what we are, including all our imperfections and inadequacies. The critical, absolutely essential question is, Can we see it? Can we be with it? Can we welcome it? Can we sit with it? Can we know it? Can we embrace our own analog, miraculous wholeness, the result of billions of years of evolution on this small planet, and embody it, here, where we already are, in the very situations, good, bad, ugly, lost, confusing, heart-rending, terrifying, and painful, that we find ourselves in?

---

* See *The Healing Power of Mindfulness*, Hachette, New York, 2018, 38–51.

Can we be the knowing that awareness already is? Can we recognize and tap into its healing potential, its wisdom and its inclusive embrace of the whole, in all its diversity and beauty, both as individuals and as a species? Can we realize the infinite beauty and mystery and intelligence of our own awareness and realize, too, that deployment of this veritable superpower can be infinitely refined through tending, through the cultivation of an affectionate and tender attention? Can we realize that wherever we go, indeed there we are, and that this "there" is always "here" and so requires at least acknowledgment and perhaps a degree of recognition and acceptance of what is, however it is, because it already is? Might it be possible now, in the only moment we ever have, to grow into ourselves in our fullness and live our precious and fleeting lives more wisely, intent on minimizing if not completely eradicating harm—from the individual to the planetary—and maximizing our own and each other's wellbeing to whatever degree imaginable and implementable?

These are all one question really. And the gut response is, We can, we can. . . . When you come right down to it, what else is there to do—for us, for our children and grandchildren and future generations, for all humanity, for the natural world, for this blue dot of a planet in the unimaginable and humbling vastness of space and time that the James Webb Space Telescope, out beyond the orbit of the moon, is revealing? If we can engineer such marvels, and marvel at what we are seeing and learning as we look ever farther into space and thus further and further back in time to close to the beginning, and ponder the mystery of consciousness and of life in a universe that apparently is only 4 percent made of the matter stuff we recognize and know a little something about—the rest being "dark matter" and "dark energy"—why can't we come to both recognize and realize that our one life—the direct outcome of 13.8 billion years of the universe coming into being and offering itself to our apprehension through sentience, through consciousness, through the mystery of awareness—is an insanely precious opportunity to dwell in amazement, in wonder, in love and compassion for the sake of our own lives and the lives of future generations, while we have the chance?

And what could be more important than to give our very life, in the fullness of its possibilities and its very actualities, often unseen, unnoticed, and unused, back to ourselves while we do have the chance? It is either "Wherever you go, there you are" or "Wherever you go, there you aren't." Both are true to a degree in any moment. But we can fiddle with the degreeness and so reclaim who and what we already are, and always have been, right here, right now . . . only temporarily forgotten. That is the practice.

Mindfulness, cultivated for even a few minutes, draws the heart toward itself. It invites the intimacy we yearn for and that is calling to us because, ultimately, mindfulness is intimacy—with ourselves and the world—underneath any apparent separation between the two. The practice immediately makes available to us both the world's and our heart's intrinsic goodness and beauty, revealing through our direct experience the power and solace of resting in the timeless present moment in awareness, out of the winds of our too-often-afflictive emotions and the agitations of an unquiet and continually judging mind. It also makes evident that these afflictive arisings cannot but abate on their own if we cease denying them or attempting to shut them down, which only feeds their disquieting energies and so often leads to harm and suffering in all directions, inwardly and outwardly, rather than to embodied wisdom and kindness. Can we take refuge in what is deepest and best and most beautiful in ourselves as human beings? I am hopeful that we can. We must. Together.

*

In 2004, while teaching in Hong Kong, I had the opportunity to go to Shenzhen, China, to visit with a highly revered ninety-eight-year-old Zen master by the name of Venerable Ben Huan at his then brand-new monastery feng shui'd seamlessly into a hillside in a beautiful park. I went with a number of MBSR colleagues from the Hong Kong Hospital Authority, and with one of Ben Huan's Dharma successors, the Venerable Hin Hung, who translated for me. Hin Hung, who I discovered had, for his own reasons, made a point of reading and thoroughly studying my scientific papers on MBSR as well as my books, explained to the master a little about MBSR and the work my colleagues and I had been doing at the hospital for, at that time, twenty-five years. In response, Ben Huan said, looking first around the room as he spoke and then straight at me, "There are an infinite number of ways in which people suffer. Therefore, there have to be an infinite number of ways in which the Dharma is made available to them." When that was translated for me, I felt a deep sense of recognition and acceptance. Gazing into his eyes, in that moment I was struck that he looked very much like my paternal grandfather. Then, again looking straight at me, he asked, smiling, "What tradition do you teach in?" He clearly wanted to push this foreigner a bit and in a friendly way test his understanding, as is the way in the Chan/Zen tradition. Figuring that I had better cover the bases, I responded, "I teach in the tradition of the Buddha and of Hui-neng." It was perhaps beyond arrogant for me to say such a thing, but it felt right in that moment. He came right back with, "What's the primary point?" and I responded, "Why nonattachment, of course." At which point, he said (this is all with Hin Hung translating and then later corroborating that I hadn't just made it up), "Would you like to become my student?" I smiled and leaned in closer to him, gazing into his eyes, and said, "I thought I already was your student." He laughed and said, "Let's go eat lunch." And so we did.

Venerable Ben Huan died ten years later, at the age of 107. Although he invited me to return, and I very much hoped that I would, it never happened. Yet I left his temple that day feeling that we were complete, that we had met beyond time and space and had touched each other in a beautiful way.*

---

* I originally told this story as part of a lengthy foreword to the book *Teaching Mindfulness: A Practical Guide for Clinicians and Educators*, by Donald McCown, Diane Reibel, and Marc S. Micozzi, Springer, New York, 2010. In that foreword, I also said, by way of providing a bit of context: "I answered Venerable Ben Huan as I did in that moment. In another place, or at another time, or under different circumstances, I might have answered very differently. In this kind of exchange in the Chan/Zen tradition, the answer itself is not important, but one's awareness of the question and where it is coming from is very important. There are plenty of responses which miss the mark completely, but there is never one right answer, just as there is no one right way to practice."

*

And so we come to the end, which is only the beginning, just as each inbreath is a new beginning and each outbreath a complete letting go. If you have come this far, the deepest of bows to you for the courage and perseverance involved in throwing yourself wholeheartedly into this adventure of a lifetime. In our everyday lives, we are all embodying and mirroring the myriad emergent forms of what might be possible for ourselves, for each other, and for the world itself, moment by moment and breath by breath. With every breath, we are continually invited to embody and therefore actualize the possible more consistently, more ardently, more compassionately, with greater appreciation for the clarity, sanity, and wellbeing that are always and already right beneath our noses, and within all of us—while we still have the chance.

May we continue to give ourselves over to what is deepest and best in ourselves, over and over and over again, encouraging those seeds of our truest nature to grow and flower and—for the sake of all beings near and far, known and unknown, and for the world in all its beauty and its anguish—nourish our lives and work and world from moment to moment and from day to day.

Jon Kabat-Zinn

Northampton, MA

Spring 2024

Resources

See https://www.jonkabat-zinn.com for Jon's guided meditations in app and digital download forms, and for his books, scientific papers, videos, and ways to connect with communities of interest doing work in the mindfulness space.

The author gratefully acknowledges permission from these sources to reprint the following:

From *I Am That: Talks with Sri Nisargadatta Maharaj*, trans. from the Marathi tape recordings by Maurice Frydman, ed. Sukhar S. Dikshit. Copyright 1973 Chetana Pvt. Ltd., Bombay. First American edition published by Acorn Press, Durham, NC, 1982, sixth printing 1992. Reprinted by permission of the American publisher.

Portions reprinted from *The Enlightened Heart*, by Stephen Mitchell (Wu-men, Chuang Tzu, Li Po, Issa, Basso, Dogen), Harper & Row, 1989.

From *The Kabir Book*, by Robert Bly. Copyright © 1971, 1977 by Robert Bly. Reprinted by permission of Beacon Press.

Martha Graham quoted in article by Agnes DeMille published in the *New York Times*, Sunday, April 7, 1991.

Portions reprinted from *Tao-te-Ching*, trans. Stephen Mitchell, HarperPerennial, 1988.

Specified excerpt from *The Practice of the Wild*, by Gary Snyder. Copyright © 1990 by Gary Snyder. Reprinted by permission of North Point Press, a division of Farrar, Straus and Giroux, Inc.

Selection reprinted from *The Joy of Insight*, by Victor Weisskopf, Basic Books, 1991.

Acknowledgments

I would like to thank Myla Kabat-Zinn, the late Sarah Doering, Larry Rosenberg, John Miller, Danielle Levi Alvares, Randy Paulsen, the late Martin Diskin, Dennis Humphrey, and the late Ferris Urbanowski for reading early drafts of the original book, so long ago, and for giving me their valuable insights and encouragement. My deep appreciation to Trudy Silverstein and the late Barry Silverstein for the use of Rocky Horse Ranch during an intensive period of early writing of the first edition, and to Jason and Wendy Cook for western adventures during those wonderful days. Profound gratitude to my original editors of thirty years ago at Hyperion, Bob Miller (now of Flatiron Books) and Mary Ann Naples (now at Hachette Books), for their deep commitment to excellence and the pleasure of working with them on the original version, and to Patricia van der Leun, my literary agent for this book from its very beginning. I also wish to thank Renée Sedliar, my kind and keen-eyed editor for this edition at Hachette Books, as well as Carrie Watterson and Cisca Schreefel for perspicacious copyediting.

Continue the journey with the full set of Jon Kabat-Zinn's four small-but-mighty guides to mindfulness and meditation, taken from his bestselling classic *Coming to Our Senses.*

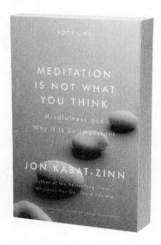

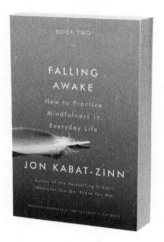

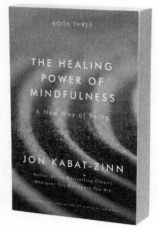

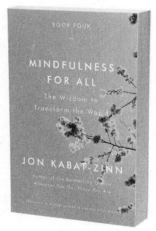

About the Author

Jon Kabat-Zinn, PhD, did his doctoral work in molecular biology at MIT in the laboratory of the Nobel laureate Salvador Luria. Jon is professor of medicine emeritus at the University of Massachusetts Medical School, where he founded its world-renowned Mindfulness-Based Stress Reduction (MBSR) Clinic in 1979, and the Center for Mindfulness in Medicine, Health Care, and Society in 1995. He is the author of fifteen books, currently in print in more than forty-five languages, and a series of research papers on MBSR dating back to 1982. In a 2021 study of trends and developments in mindfulness research over fifty-five years (1966–2021), three of his empirical studies are among the ten most cited articles on mindfulness (nos. 3, 5, and 9) in the scientific literature, and a review article he authored is number 2 among citations of the top 10 review articles on mindfulness. His work and that of his colleagues in the United States and around the world have contributed to a vibrant and growing movement of mindfulness into mainstream institutions such as medicine; psychology; health care; neuroscience; sustainability research; schools; higher education; business; racial, social, and economic justice; criminal justice; prisons; the law; technology; police; the military; government; and professional sports. More than seven hundred hospitals and medical centers around the world now offer MBSR. Jon lectures and leads mindfulness workshops and retreats around the world, in person and online. In early 2020, as the COVID-19 pandemic was growing exponentially, he offered a three-month "mitigation retreat" online, consisting of sixty-six consecutive weekdays of live ninety-minute sessions, including guided meditations, talks, and dialogue, with several thousand people joining each day. Those sessions can be accessed at https://www.youtube.com/playlist?list =PL5kRdSV9ccDmlkq9lamDtu4PmnXN9Lxrj.

For more information on Jon and on mindfulness in action on planet Earth, visit www.jonkabat-zinn.com.